THE
BOOK
from THE SITE

THE

BOOK

from THE SITE

Lennard Publishing

First edition published in 1997 by
Lennard Publishing
a division of Lennard Associates
Mackerye End, Harpenden
Herts AL5 5DR

ISBN 1 85291 131 X

British Library Cataloguing in Publication
Data is available

Editor: Kirsty Ennever
Production Editor: Chris Hawkes
Cover design by Paul Cooper
Text design by Forest Publication Services

Printed and bound in Great Britain by
Clays Ltd, St Ives plc

CONTENTS

ACKNOWLEDGEMENTS

We are grateful to Tomkins plc, The Duke of Edinburgh's Award and Sir Harry and Lady Solomon through whose generous support it has been possible to distribute a complimentary copy of *The Book* to every secondary school, college of further education and university in the UK.

Other supporters of *The Site*:

Barclays Bank plc
British Airways
BT
Coca-Cola Youth Foundation
Coopers and Lybrand
Crockers Oswald Hickson
GrandMet
Halifax plc
Hulton Getty Picture Collection
Hillsdown Holdings
IBM
Imperial College, London
Joseph Levy Charitable
    Foundation
Leopold Muller Estate

Lloyds TSB Foundation
Marks & Spencer
Microsoft
NatWest
Netscape
Oracle Corporation UK Ltd
Sherman Foundation
Sun Microsystems
National Lottery Charities Board
UKERNA
Walt Disney Company
Web Development
Web Media

FOREWORD

Every young person's life is shaped by the help and advice they are given in those early years of growing up. But too often that advice is based on the limited knowledge of the last (perhaps the only) person they spoke to. Many parents, tackled by an enquiring teenager, have difficulty knowing just where to begin. Even teachers and youth workers who specialise in such advice might offer contact advice details of three or four organisations in a particular field; they might not know of dozens of others, some much more appropriate to the young person's needs.

Go For It! began as an annual publication four years ago – then, as now, delivered free, through generous business sponsorship, to all secondary schools, universities and colleges of higher and further education – with the aim of removing the 'hit and miss' element of that all-important early search for help and advice. It remains the most comprehensive, user-friendly guidebook to every form of opportunity and help a young person growing up in Britain today might need. No fewer than 700 key organisations offering information, help and advice are easily accessible either by name or category.

This year, for the first time, *Go For It!* (re-named *The Book*) is proud to reveal the existence of a 'big sister'! It has been clear that there are thousands of smaller, local organisations in Britain, stretching right down to community level, which young people might wish to access. They are far too numerous to be included in this book – but they can be comprehensively listed on the Internet, where a new charity, YouthNet, has been busy gathering them up on a web site which is called simply and memorably *The Site* (http://www.thesite.org.uk). It is a product of extensive consultation and agreement throughout the youth sector, centralising and cross-checking for the first time basic information which was previously only available on a wide range of databases with differing priorities. An electronic signpost designed by young people themselves, it uses state-of-the-art search mechanisms to make it easy to narrow the options among the many thousands of entries. All you have to do is tap in your postcode, area of interest, and the distance you are prepared to travel to pursue that interest, and – within seconds – you are offered a brief description and contact details of the relevant organisations. Soon you should also be able to print out a map showing you how to get there.

Finally, on behalf of the splendid YouthNet team, can I express our enormous gratitude to The National Lottery Charities Board and our rapidly growing army of corporate supporters and charity partners who have helped make all this possible. And for those of you about to launch yourselves into *The Book* or *The Site* itself, I wish you good hunting. You are but a few seconds away from the definitive first port of call not just for young people, but for all who care about them.

Martyn Lewis CBE
Founder and Chairman of YouthNet
November 1997

INTRODUCING THE SITE

Launched in January 1997, *The Site* (http://www.thesite.org.uk) is an interactive Internet-based guide to the huge range of opportunities, help and advice available to young people. As it develops, *The Site* will become a natural first port of call for information, taking the gamble out of making the right choices, both in seeking help when needed and in taking positive decisions about the future.

Making it easy and natural to use has been a priority. Whether looking for advice on a problem or trying to find a job, *The Site* covers it all in a style and format relevant to young people. There is no jargon and there is a help section if you need it.

The issues covered reflect what users have told us is important. Information on Drugs, Education, Freetime, Health, Housing, Money, Sex, Sport and Work are all included. As *The Book* goes to the printers there are over 12,000 records of people who can help and it grows every day. We are also developing a number of highly creative projects with partners like The Duke of Edinburgh's Award to make *The Site* both innovative and fun as well.

Probably the most important aspect of how we have designed *The Site* is the ability to search in a number of different ways. A post-code mapping system is built in to help you find sources of help within a specified radius of where you live – it's the local people you want to find, not just national organisations. This makes *The Site* unique and particularly relevant in areas like volunteering, job hunting and counselling.

There is so much good information available, held in many different databases. The last thing we want to do is research it all again. We have a growing number of information partners, usually charities themselves, and we pool all this content together in one place and make it easily searchable. This, together with our own research to fill in the gaps, is what enables us to have such a diverse and comprehensive resource.

To explore *The Site* all you need is access to the Internet. With the drive to have all schools and libraries on-line, as well as the growing number of homes with computers, access is increasing all the time. We are also working to make *The Site*'s information available on the new digital broadcasting TVs coming into service next year.

While *The Site* is designed for young people, it can make life easier for anyone bombarded with requests for information and help. Youth workers, careers' advisers, parents – all will find this an invaluable resource.

You can visit *The Site* at this address: http://www. thesite.org.uk

INTRODUCING THE BOOK

The Book from *The Site* follows the structure of *The Site* almost identically, making it very easy to use. There are nine sections in *The Book*:

Advice includes advice centres, bereavement, helplines, law matters, money, race, relationships and special needs.

Drugs includes information and help centres specialising in alcohol and drugs problems.

Education includes training and courses and links to universities and FE colleges.

Freetime is the largest chapter in the book. This section includes adventure and sport, arts, awards and competitions, clubs and groups, conservation and nature, expeditions, volunteering organisations, working abroad and holiday work.

Health includes AIDS/HIV, care and carers, general health and mental health.

Housing includes information for care leavers, finding accommodation, homelessness and housing rights.

Sex includes gay and lesbian organisations, sexual health and victim support.

Work includes advice centres, careers, employment and setting up your own business, plus information on CVs and interview techniques.

WWW has listings of some of the coolest

web sites around for computing, film and TV, games, Internet, music, news, screen savers and travel.

The Site *contains thousands of local organisations. For* The Book, *we chose mostly national organisations, ensuring that the information held is relevant to whoever is using it, wherever they are in the UK. These national organisations will be able to give you details of your local branch when you get in touch with them.*

To help you find your way around *The Book,* there is an alphabetical listing of every organisation in *The Book* in an index at the back and also an alphabetical listing for every organisation in each chapter in the 'Finding Your Way Around' section.

In keeping with the structure of *The Site,* each section divides its content into organisations, publications, information and web sites.

We very much hope you find *The Book* useful and a good read and hope you enjoy surfing *The Site.*

In recent years The Duke of Edinburgh's Award has grown into one of the most widely respected programmes for personal development available for people aged between 14 and 25. With over 120,000 participants in the UK alone, the Award has an innovative approach to providing great opportunities for anyone who has a go at one (or all) of its three levels: Bronze, Silver and Gold. Part of this approach is to use the Internet to reach even more people than ever thought possible – thus empowering participants through the use of new technology.

This has resulted in a new partnership between YouthNet and the Award in implementing a dynamic new area on *The Site*. Over the next year we will be developing an interactive Award presence, as well as information on just about anything you can think of to do with freetime opportunities. So if you want to know more about conservation or volunteering or even working abroad *The Site* and The Duke of Edinburgh's Award can help you in your search for something to do. From arts to adventure – it's all easy to find on *The Site*.

FINDING
YOUR
WAY
AROUND

Advice

Organisations

Publications

Web Sites

Drugs

Education & Educational Exchanges

Organisation

THE
BOOK

Publications

Information

Web Sites

Freetime

ADVENTURE & SPORT

Organisations

ARTS

Organisations

AWARDS & COMPETITIONS

Organisations

CLUBS & GROUPS

Organisations

CONSERVATION & NATURE

Organisations

Publications

EXPEDITIONS

Organisations

WORKING ABROAD & HOLIDAY WORK

Organisations

Publications

Web Sites

Health

Organisations

Housing

Organisations

Sex

Organisations

Web Sites

Work

Organisations

WWW

Computing

Film & TV

Fun, Games & Screen Savers

ADVICE

THE
BOOK

ADVICE

Groups served
Parents/carers of children up to the age of 11
and children with special needs up to the age
of 19

Address	Wyndhams
	St Josephs Place
	Devizes
	Wiltshire SN10 1DD
Telephone	0345 585 072
Fax	01380 728 476

ANTI-BULLYING CAMPAIGN

Helpline

Telephone helpline offering support and
advice for parents whose children have been
bullied at school. Offers advice on how to
help children, what steps to take with the
school and the education system. Has fact
sheets for sale. Offers training to teachers and
pupils.

Groups served

Parents whose children have been bullied at
school

Address	185 Tower Bridge Road
	London SE1 2UF
Telephone	0171 378 1446
Fax	0171 378 8374

ORGANISATIONS

ADVICE

ARIB – AFRICA RESEARCH AND INFORMATION BUREAU

Forum made up of African refugees, migrants and students. Advice on immigration and welfare rights, training in computer literacy, job search skills and interview techniques. Range of information and research about Africa/African refugees.

Groups served
African refugees and migrants
Address   2nd Floor
                   5 Westminster Bridge Road
                   London SE1 7XW
Telephone   0171 928 8728
Fax   0171 928 8728

ASK – ADVICE ON SERVICES FOR KIDS

Advice and information on services for children up to the age of 11 and children and young people with special needs up to the age of 19. Telephone helpline every weekday morning gives advice and information on education, child care, learning disabilities and local resources. Also produces leaflets on specific topics to do with the education system.

BENEFITS OFFICES

Provides benefits and benefit information

Benefits agencies' primary role is the administration and payment of 22 social security benefits including income support, incapacity benefit, severe disablement allowance, maternity allowance, family credit, child benefit, disability living allowance and social fund crisis loans.

How to contact
The organisation has no main telephone number. To find your local office look in your telephone directory or call directory enquiries

CAPA (CIVIL RIGHTS ADVICE & SUPPORT GROUP)

Racial and domestic violence

Provides advice, support and information to survivors of racial violence and domestic violence. 24-hour advice and information line.

Groups served
Survivors of racial violence and domestic violence

Address　　　　St Hilda's Community Centre
　　　　　　　　　18 Club Row
　　　　　　　　　London E2 7EY
Telephone　　　0171 729 2652 (helpline)

CARELINE

Telephone counselling

Confidential telephone counselling. Issues dealt with include: family, marital and relationship problems, child abuse, bullying, sexual abuse, rape, bereavement, HIV/AIDS, addictions, stress, depression, loneliness and anxiety etc.

Groups served
General public

Address	Cardinal Heenan Centre
	326 High Road
	Ilford IG1 1QP
Telephone	0181 514 1177 (counselling)
Fax	0181 478 7943

CHILDLINE

Telephone helpline

Free 24-hour helpline for children and young people in danger, distress or with any problem. Offers telephone counselling, support, advice and referrals. ChildLine for children in care: 0800 44 44 6pm-10pm every day.

Groups served
Children and young people

ADVICE

Address	2nd Floor, Royal Mail Building
	Studd Street
	London N1 0QW
Telephone	0800 1111 (helpline)

CHILDREN'S LEGAL CENTRE – ADVICE LINE

Telephone advice, information and, where appropriate, referrals to other relevant agencies on all issues about the law as it affects children, including local authority care.

Groups served
Children, parents and professionals involved with children

Address	University of Essex
	Wivenhoe Park
	Colchester
	Essex CO4 3SQ
Telephone	01206 873820
Fax	01206 874026

CITIZEN'S ADVICE BUREAU

There are over 7,000 bureaux around the country who can advise you on issues including benefits, debt, education, employment, health, housing, immigration, legal matters, relationships and tax. To find your local bureau, phone directory enquiries or contact their main office below.

Address	Myddelton House
	115-123 Pentonville Road
	London N1 9LZ
Telephone	0171 833 2181
Fax	0171 833 4371

CITIZENSHIP FOUNDATION, THE

Independent educational charity directed to helping young people, in particular, to become involved and effective citizens. Through a variety of programmes, including the development of materials, it aims to develop knowledge and understanding of the legal, social and democratic systems. Practical activities such as mock trials and mock parliament competitions help to promote self esteem and communication skills. The charity tries to target those who often feel excluded. Programmes now in Central and Eastern Europe. Award scheme in

Northern Ireland and the Republic. Long term aim to establish a series of community-based groups/networks to develop local programmes. Strong school base throughout the age range.

Address	15 St Swithin's Lane
	London EC4N 8AL
Telephone	0171 929 3344
Fax	0171 929 9922
E-mail	citfou@gn.apc.org

COMMISSION FOR RACIAL EQUALITY (HEAD OFFICE)

Head office of the CRE, which works towards the elimination of racial discrimination, promotes equal opportunities and good race relations, enforces the Race Relations Act 1976 and monitors how it is working. There are regional offices across the country and local Race Equality Councils that carry out case work in relation to matters of racial discrimination and harassment.

Groups served
General public

Address	Elliot House
	20 Allington Street
	London SW1E 5EH
Telephone	0171 828 7022
Fax	0171 630 9680

CRISIS COUNSELLING FOR ALLEGED SHOPLIFTERS

Volunteer-run service offering counselling, advice, support and assistance, including referrals to other agencies/professionals, for alleged shoplifters. Booklet available for £1.50.

Groups served
People accused of alleged shoplifting offences
Address   PO Box 147
              Stanmore
              Middlesex HA7 4YT
Telephone   0181 958 8859

ERITREAN COMMUNITY IN THE UK

Advice and information for the Eritrean community on benefits, employment, education and housing. Women's groups and supplementary schools, range of cultural and social activities.

Groups served
The Eritrean community
Address   266-268 Holloway Road
              London N7 6NE
Telephone   0171 700 7995

FAMILY MEDIATION SERVICE – INSTITUTE OF FAMILY THERAPY

Mediators help couples who are separating or divorced to resolve disagreements relating to contact and residence of children and financial matters. The service is also available to children of separating parents. There is a sliding scale of charges for users of the service.

Groups served
Any parent who is separating or divorcing
Address   24-32 Stephenson Way
                 London NW1 2HX
Telephone   0171 391 9150
Fax   0171 391 9169

IMMIGRATION ADVISORY SERVICE – LONDON

Advice and representation for people experiencing difficulties or problems with immigration and asylum. Representation at immigration tribunals and appeals. Offers a walk-in service from 9.30am Monday/Tuesday/Thursday and Friday to first 40 people. Also runs a 24-hour helpline on 0171 378 9191.

Groups served
Immigrants to the UK, including asylum seekers

Address	County House
	190 Great Dover Street
	London SE1 4YB
Telephone	0171 357 6917
Fax	0171 403 5875

INDIAN MUSLIM FEDERATION (UK)

Advice and information on benefits, employment, homelessness, housing rights, immigration and money/debt. Elderly luncheon club, various activities for Asian women, youth activities, mother tongue classes for 6-14-year-olds.

Groups served
The local Asian community

Address	Indian Muslim Federation Hall
	Trinity Close
	London E11 4RP
Telephone	0181 558 6399

INTERNATIONAL SOCIAL SERVICE OF THE UK

International social work organisation providing an inter-country service for members of the public and agencies. Deals with issues that require the cooperation of social workers and other agencies in other countries. Also provides an international

ADVICE

tracing service for relatives, advice for people wishing to return to their country of origin and a foreign marriage advice service.

Groups served
General public, social workers, court welfare, probation services etc

Address	Cranmer House
	39 Brixton Road
	London SW9 6DD
Telephone	0171 735 8941
Fax	0171 582 0696

LAW CENTRES FEDERATION (LCF)

Provide a free and independent professional legal service

Law centres were set up to overcome the obstacles faced by people who need access to the legal system. Free, publicly provided legal advice should be available to everyone, not just those with financial resources or those few who can get legal aid. Even if a person were able to qualify for legal aid because of their income, there are many areas of the law where legal aid is simply not available. This means that even in areas where fundamental rights are in dispute there is no access to the legal system. Law Centres provide a more complete and responsive service to people than the individual service provided by private lawyers. This means providing a more efficient and comprehensive service for their users.

Address	Duchess House
	18-19 Warren House
	London W1P 5DB
Telephone	0171 387 8570
Fax	0171 387 8363

MASH (MEN AS SURVIVORS HELPLINE)

Male survivors of sexual abuse

Telephone counselling and advice service for men who have been raped or sexually abused at any time in their lives, their families and friends.

Groups served
Males who have been raped or sexually abused, their families and friends

Address	c/o Victim Support
	36 Dean Lane
	Bedminster
	Bristol BS1 1BS
Telephone	0117 907 7100

ADVICE

NAC FOUNDATION CENTRE

Offenders' support

Resource centre offering rehabiliation and training services to offenders, ex-offenders, those at risk of offending and young people with special educational needs. Structured 12-week programme and personalised training plans.

Groups served
Offenders, ex-offenders (aged between 17 and 35), young people with special educational needs

Address	62-64 Culvert Road
	Battersea
	London SW11 5AR
Telephone	0171 924 3974

NCH ACTION FOR CHILDREN

National office of NCH Action for Children, a voluntary child care organisation with projects across Britain. Services include: family centres, respite care for children with disabilities, alternative to custody schemes for young offenders and supported housing for care leavers.

Groups served
Children at risk and in need and their families

Address	85 Highbury Park
	London N5 1UD
Telephone	0171 226 2033

NSPCC – NATIONAL CHILD PROTECTION HELPLINE

Helpline for anyone concerned about a child at risk of abuse, including children themselves. Counselling, information and advice. Staffed by social work counsellors.

Groups served
People concerned about a child at risk of abuse, including children themselves

Address	42 Curtain Road
	London
	EC2A 3NH
Telephone	0800 800 500 (helpline)
Fax	0171 825 2790

NATIONAL ASSOCIATION FOR THE CARE AND RESETTLEMENT OF OFFENDERS (NACRO)

NACRO provides information and help to people who have been in trouble with the law and those at risk of becoming so. They provide information and help with employment and training, housing, prisons and resettlement and the law. NACRO also

ADVICE

operates youth activities for those living in deprived and disadvantaged areas.

Address	169 Clapham Road Stockwell London SW9 0PU
Telephone	0171 582 6500
Fax	0171 735 4666

NATIONAL DEBTLINE

National telephone helpline for people with debt problems. Gives expert advice over the phone and sends callers in debt a self-help information pack free of charge.

Groups served
People with money problems

Address	Birmingham Settlement 318 Summer Lane Birmingham B19 3RL
Telephone	0645 500 51
Fax	0121 359 6357

NATIONAL MISSING PERSONS HELPLINE

Telephone support service offering counselling, listening and practical support to anyone with a missing relative or immediate family member. Runs a national computerised register of missing persons.

THE BOOK

Groups served
Anyone with a missing relative or immediate
family member

Address   Roebuck House
                  284-286 Upper Richmond
                  Road West
                  London SW14 7JE
Telephone   0500 700 700 (freephone)
Minicom   9181 878 7752

ADVICE

NATIONAL STEPFAMILY ASSOCIATION

National advice, information and support for
all members of stepfamilies and those who
work with them. Telephone counselling
service, training, publications and a quarterly
newsletter.

Groups served
Those living in stepfamilies

Address   Chapel House
                  18 Hatton Place
                  London EC1N 8RU
Telephone   0990 168 388
                  (counselling helpline)
Fax   0171 209 2461

OFF THE RECORD

Advice/counselling

Advice, information and counselling services for young people up to 25 years of age. Also sexual health clinic. Topics covered include: housing, homelessness, sexual health, employment, drugs, HIV/AIDS. Legal advice by appointment.

Groups served
Young people up to 25 years of age living, working or studying in Richmond

Address   2 Church Street
            Twickenham
            Middlesex TW1 3NY
Telephone   0181 744 1644

POSITIVE DISCOUNTS

Discounts on items from food to travel and entertainment in the UK and abroad. Positive Discounts enable anyone to obtain discounts in thousands of shops and on services throughout the UK and abroad. Discounts can be obtained on food, travel, insurance, places of entertainment, in thousands of shops thoughout the UK and abroad.

Costs
The scheme is free to anyone who is HIV+,

people on benefits or mandatory student grants. For everyone else, the subscription is £10 per year

Address   PO Box 347
                 Twickenham
                 Middlesex TW1 2SN
Telephone   0181 891 2561
Fax   0181 408 3081
E-mail
hello@positive-discounts.org.uk
Web site
http://www.positive-discounts.org.uk

PRISON LINK

Provides advice, support and befriending to prisoners and their families. Offers a range of services – transport, counselling, a children's club, access to accommodation and annual summer camps. Part of the United Evangelical Project.

Groups served
Prisoners and their families
Address   29 Trinity Road
                 Aston
                 Birmingham B6 6AJ
Telephone   0121 551 1207
Fax   0121 554 4894

ADVICE

PRISONERS' WIVES AND FAMILIES SOCIETY

Information, advice and support for families and friends of prisoners, covering housing, benefits, debt, homelessness and legal issues.

Groups served
Families and friends of prisoners
Address   254 Caledonian Road
                  London N1 0NG
Telephone   0171 278 3981

RNID – SOUTH EAST & HQ

Regional office providing information on all aspects of deafness for deaf people, their families and professionals. Offers interpreting services, training, specialist telephone services, environmental aids and runs residential care projects. Campaigns to remove discrimination and prejudice.

Groups served
Deaf, deafened, hard of hearing and deaf-blind people, their families and friends
How to contact
Voice phone, textphone or write
Address   19-23 Featherstone Street
                  London EC1Y 8SL
Telephone   0870 6050123

RELATE (HEAD OFFICE)

Coordinates local Relate Centres in England, Wales and Northern Ireland. The Centres offer counselling for adults with relationship difficulties, whether married or not. Some Centres offer psychosexual counselling and mediation. Publishes a range of literature available by mail order. Payment for counselling or therapy is according to income.

Groups served
Adult couples with relationship difficulties

Address	Herbert Gray College
	Little Church Street
	Rugby CV21 3AP
Telephone	01788 573241
Fax	01788 535007

RIGHTS OF WOMEN

Legal advice for women

Advice and information for women on a range of legal issues – relationship breakdown and childcare issues, lesbian parenting, domestic violence, sexual violence or harassment, employment rights. Will take calls from women across the UK but cannot advise on Scottish law.

ADVICE

Groups served
Women
Address   52-54 Featherstone Street
                  London EC1Y 8RT
Telephone   0171 251 6577 (advice)
Fax   0171 608 0928

WOMEN'S DOMESTIC VIOLENCE HELPLINE

Confidential helpline providing telephone counselling, advice, information on domestic violence, welfare rights, finding alternative accommodation and legal services. Makes referrals to refuges and safe houses, solicitors and other agencies who can offer support. Also offers advice to other agencies about domestic violence.

Groups served
Women experiencing domestic violence. Also agencies working with women
Address   PO Box 156
                  Newton Street
                  Manchester M60 1DB
Telephone   0161 839 8574

PUBLICATIONS

GRANTS FOR INDIVIDUALS IN NEED, A GUIDE TO

Charities concerned with individual poverty

A guide to more than 2,100 charities concerned with individual poverty.

For further information please contact:

	The Directory of Social Change
	24 Stephenson Way
	London NW1 9LZ
Telephone	0171 209 5151
Fax	0171 209 5049
Price	£16.95
ISBN	1 90036 001 2

WEB SITES

BENEFITS AGENCIES

A large government listing of benefits agencies

Web site
http://www.dss.gov.uk/ba

MONEY WORLD GUIDE TO PERSONAL FINANCE

Q&As and guides to who offers what from banking to pensions

Web site
http://www.moneyworld.co.uk/ukpfd/

PENAL LEXICON

Information on prisons and the penal system in England, Wales and Northern Ireland

Web site
http://www.penlex.org.uk

DRUGS

DRUGS

ORGANISATIONS

ADFAM NATIONAL

Drug helpline

A national telephone helpline for the families and friends of drug users, offering advice, information and support. Also offers training to workers developing drug-related family support projects nationwide.

Groups served
Families and friends of drug users and those working with them

Address	5th Floor, Epworth House
	25 City Road
	London EC1Y 1AA
Telephone	0171 928 8900

AL-ANON FAMILY GROUPS UK AND EIRE

Alcohol support

Understanding and support for families and friends of problem drinkers, whether the person is still drinking or not. Contact for details of meetings throughout the UK and Eire.

Groups served
Families and friends of problem drinkers

Address	61 Great Dover Street
	London SE1 4YF
Telephone	0171 403 0888
	(24-hour helpline)

ALATEEN

Young people, alcohol problems

Part of Al-Anon Family Groups. Offers support to young people aged between 12 and 20 affected by someone else's drinking – usually that of a parent.

Groups served
Teenagers affected by somebody else's drinking – usually a parent

Address	61 Great Dover Street
	London SE1 4YF
Telephone	0171 403 0888

ALCOHOLICS ANONYMOUS (LONDON)

Confidential helpline for people with drink problems staffed by recovering alcoholics. Can give details of when local AA groups meet. Open 365 days a year and can arrange contact with a local member.

Groups served
People with drink problems

DRUGS

Address   London Region Telephone
Service
1st Floor
11 Redcliffe Gardens
London SW10 9BG
Telephone 0171 352 3001

DRINKLINE

Telephone helpline

Helpline offering advice, information and support to anyone concerned about their own or someone else's drinking. Referrals to appropriate local services. 24-hour dial-and-listen service on 0500 801 802. Asian Line Monday 1-8pm (Hindi, Urdu, Gujarati and Punjabi), dial-and-listen service in Hindi and Urdu 0990 133 480 (24 hours). Youth Line dial-and-listen service 0990 143 275 (24 hours).

Groups served
Anyone concerned about their own or someone else's drinking

Address   Petersham House
57a Hatton Garden
London EC1N 8HP
Telephone 0171 332 0202 (London)
0345 32 0202 (UK)
Fax   0171 520 5310

DRINKLINE YOUTH

Advice on alcohol

Offering advice on alcohol through a helpline, publications and the media. It consists of a confidential helpline and a dial-and-listen service of recorded information for young people. Helpline for the UK 0345 320202 – open Monday to Friday from 11am-11pm. London-only helpline 0171 332 0202. Dial and listen 0990 143 275. 24 hours, seven days a week. There are two publications available from Drinkline, *Message in a Bottle* and *Big Blue Book of Booze.*

Groups served
Young people who want help and advice on alcohol

Address	7th Floor Weddel House
	13-14 West Smithfield
	London EC1A 9DL
Telephone	0345 320202

DRUGS IN SCHOOLS HELPLINE

Service run by Release (see separate entry) and offering information, advice and referrals to specialist agencies on a range of drug-related issues for children, pupils, parents, teachers and school governors.

DRUGS

Groups served
Anyone concerned about or involved in a
drug-related incident at a school

Address	Release
	388 Old Street
	London EC1V 9LT
Telephone	0345 36 66 66

NATIONAL ASSOCIATION FOR CHILDREN OF ALCOHOLICS

Helpline

Helpline for the children (including grown-up
children) of alcoholics, professionals and
carers who work with them. Offers
information, advice and telephone
counselling.

Groups served
Children (including grown-up children) of
alcoholics

Address	PO Box 64
	Fishponds, Bristol BS16 2UH
Telephone	0800 289 061 (freephone)
Fax	0117 924 8005

NATIONAL DRUGS HELPLINE

Helpline for anyone concerned about drug
misuse, including drug users, their families,

friends and carers. Offers information, advice and counselling about all aspects of drug misuse. Also referrals to local agencies.

Groups served

Drug users, their families, friends and carers, anyone concerned about drug use

Address	PO Box 5000
	Glasgow G12 8BR
Telephone	0800 776 600 (freephone)
Fax	0141 334 0299

RELEASE

Drugs advice

Telephone information, advice and counselling to drug users and those who care for them, particularly on legal issues. Offers 24-hour emergency/crisis service via out-of-hours helpline. Education and training for statutory and voluntary agencies. Outreach workers.

Groups served

Drugs users, their families, friends and professionals dealing with related issues

Address	388 Old Street
	London EC1V 9LT
Telephone	0171 603 8654 (helpline)
Fax	0171 729 2599

DRUGS

WEB SITES

DRUG INFORMATION

Comprehensive list of all types of drugs including description, use and abuse

Web site
http://www.firstlab.com/druginfo.html

DRUG RELATED STREET TERMS/SLANG NAMES

Complete listing of all drug-related slang words matched with the official drug

Web site
http://www.addictions.com/slang.htm

INSTITUTE FOR THE STUDY OF DRUG DEPENDENCY

A wealth of information on drugs – use and abuse – and help organisations

Web site
http://www.isdd.co.uk

EDUCATION &
EDUCATIONAL
EXCHANGES

ORGANISATIONS

ADVISORY CENTRE FOR EDUCATION (ACE)

Independent, national education advice centre for parents on all aspects of the state school system. Provides training and support to community advice workers and parent groups so that they can give education advice. In addition to a regular advice line, the centre also runs an 'Exclusion from School' line on 0171 704 9822 and a line specifically for parents in the London Borough of Islington on 0171 704 2776.

Groups served
Parents of school age children

Address	1b Aberdeen Studios
	22-24 Highbury Grove
	London N5 2DQ
Telephone	0171 354 8321
Fax	0171 354 9069

AIESEC

Offers training and experience to students through international exchanges

AIESEC provides skills training with partner companies, practical experience through the organisation of projects and seminars which

EDUCATION

contributes to international youth issues such as enterprise education, learning and corporate citizenship. It also organises international exchanges, work – voluntary or education related – through its 87 country network. Entirely student run, interested students can join at any of the 25 universities where AIESEC runs as a student society.

Address   UK Office
                 29-31 Cowper Street
                 London EC2H 4AP
Telephone 0171 336 7939
Fax   0171 336 7939
E-mail
aiesec@clava.net
Web site
http://www.new.ox.ac.uk/~nick/AIESEC/main.html

EDUCATION

ASSOCIATION OF COMMONWEALTH UNIVERSITIES (ACU)

Provides information about Commonwealth universities – what the universities are like, where they are, what courses are on offer and what entrance qualifications are needed. Administers several scholarship schemes for Commonwealth university students, mainly at postgraduate level.

How to contact

Reference library at the address below open to the public on application Monday-Friday 9.30am-1pm and 2pm-5.30pm

Address   John Foster House
                     36 Gordon Square
                     London WC1H 0PF
Telephone   0171 387 8572
Fax   0171 387 2655
E-mail
pubinf@acu.ac.uk

ASSOCIATION OF JEWISH SIXTH-FORMERS (AJ6)

A Jewish peer-led organisation for fifth and sixth formers

AJ6 is the representative body of Jewish Students of fifth- and sixth-form ages, regardless of political or religious affiliations. Working to prepare its members for university life, it produces the *AJ6 Campus Guide*, runs seminars on topics of Jewish interest, takes school assemblies, runs local meetings and regularly mails out the group's magazine and news of forthcoming events. AJ6 runs summer tours to Israel, organises social events, weekends and specialist seminars, and a National Conference with emphasis on fun and education.

Numbers passing through
c1,000 members. c1,500 use services
Membership
£5.00
AJ6 publish *AJ6 Guide to Jewish Student Life* and produce a bi-monthly magazine *Sixth Sense*

Address	Hillel House
	1-2 Endsleigh Street
	London WC1H0DS
Telephone	0171 387 3384
Fax	0171 387 3392

E-mail
aj6.hq@ort.org

BROADCAST JOURNALISM TRAINING COUNCIL (BJTC)

Provides information on careers and courses in all areas of journalism

A voluntary organisation with representatives from all sides of the broadcasting industry, the NUJ and universities and colleges running recognised courses in broadcast journalism. The council's role, on behalf of the industry, is to liaise with universities and colleges to ensure that industry standards of training are maintained. Periodic visits are made to courses and recognition granted to those which conform to the council's guidelines. The NCTBJ has played, and will continue to play, a major role in the establishment of the new National Vocational Qualifications and is represented on Skillset, the industry training organisation responsible for the development of NVQs. The National Council publishes *A Future in Broadcast Journalism*, a guide to training and careers in broadcasting journalism, including a list of recognised courses and courses seeking recognition. Up to five copies sent free on application from individuals, educational institutions, careers advice services etc. More than five copies @ 5p each, including p&p.

Address	The Coach House
	2 North Road
	West Bridgford
	Nottingham NG2 7NH
Telephone	0115 945 5119
Fax	0115 945 5871

BUSINESS TRAINING AND ADVISORY SERVICE (BTAS)

Provides business training to individuals in a range of programmes

BTAS is aimed at providing the best in business training and offers its services to individuals with a range of programmes, both off the shelf and tailored to clients' specific requirements.

Courses aimed at individuals include accounting, marketing, banking, credit management and legal programmes.

Address	Hendon College
	Corner Mead
	Colindale
	London NW9 5RA
Telephone	0181 205 9219
Fax	0181 200 9220

CENTRAL BUREAU FOR EDUCATIONAL VISITS AND EXCHANGES

The Central Bureau is the UK national office responsible for information and advice on all forms of educational visits and exchanges. They do not arrange visits or exchanges for individuals, but publish books that will be able to put you in touch with the right people.

Publications
Working Holidays – £9.99
A Year Between – £8.99
Home from Home – £8.99
Volunteer Work – £8.99
Workplace – £9.99
Discovering Germany – £5.99
Regional addresses
Scotland: 3 Bruntsfield Crescent, Edinburgh
EH10 4HD Tel: 0131 447 8024
Fax: 0131 452 8569

EDUCATION

Northern Ireland: 1 Chlorine Gardens, Belfast BT9 5BN Tel: 01232 664418 Fax: 01232 661275

Address Seymour Mews House
10 Spring Gardens
London SW1A 2BN

Telephone 0171 389 4004
Fax 0171 389 4426
E-mail
info@centralbureau.org.uk
Web site
http://www.britcoun.org/cbeve

CESA LANGUAGES ABROAD

Organises language courses abroad

CESA offers an information and advice service on language courses abroad, mainly within the European Community, (ie France, Spain, Italy, Germany, Portugal and Greece) but they also work with colleges in China, Mexico, Russia and Japan. If interested in other countries please ask! You can choose between taking a very intensive language course, or more of a 'holiday' course with lessons in the morning and plenty of free time or organised activities ie French and Skiing in Mégève, German and Skiing in Kitzbühel, Spanish and Flamenco in Malaga or Italian and Art History or Drawing classes in Florence – all of which can only add to the enjoyment of your stay.

Three months plus programmes allow students to study for the State-recognised Diplomas at various centres eg DELF or CCIP qualifications in France, the Goethe Institute exams in Germany or the DELE in Spain. Once you have talked through your options and decided on a course, CESA can make all the necessary arrangements from reserving your place in the language school of your choice, to arranging whichever type of accommodation you need for your stay. CESA is a member of IALTA (International Association of Language Travel Agents).

Age range
12+ – French, Spanish and German courses only (all linguistic levels)
16+ – All languages (all linguistic levels)
Costs/waiting lists
Costs vary depending on country, length of stay, time of the year and type of course, eg short term courses: France – 20 hours of tuition and half-board family accommodation costs approx £600 for two weeks. Germany approximately the same price, Japan is more expensive, Spain, Italy, Portugal and Greece etc are cheaper. Long term courses: Spain – 20 hours of tuition and half-board family accommodation costs approx £3,400 for a six-month programme. Travel costs are not included in the course fees and most students make their own arrangements, but CESA

EDUCATION

willingly offers advice on travel options. Waiting lists are not a problem as programmes are run throughout the year. However, be warned – July and August are very busy months and need to be booked well in advance. CESA publish a variety of free leaflets, *French Course Abroad*, *Spanish Course Abroad*, *German Courses Abroad*, *Gap Year Language Courses* and *How to Study Abroad*

Address   Western House
                 Malpas
                 Truro
                 Cornwall TR1 1SQ
Telephone   01872 225300
Fax   01872 225400
E-mail
languages@cesa.demon.co.uk

CHALLENGE EDUCATIONAL SERVICES

Provides French language and USA work placement programmes

Challenge Educational Services offers students the opportunity to learn or perfect their French language skills and learn about the French way of life and culture. Intensive, general and tailor-made courses to suit all levels – plus private homestay, French for business, A-level revision and summer programmes – accommodation on full or half board included.

Students can study at the prestigious Sorbonne University, Paris, or the University of Angers, Nantes, Poitiers or Toulouse for a semester (5 months), academic year (10 months) or during the summer (4-6 weeks).

Students aged between 15 and 18 can spend 5-10 months at an American high school anywhere in the USA – an opportunity to combine academic and sporting activities, learn about the American way of life and culture at first hand.

Challenge Educational Services offers graduates and undergraduates aged between 18 and 26 the unique opportunity to gain quality work experience in their chosen field of study in an American business for 2-3 months in San Francisco.

Participants gain an insight into the methods and strategies of an American business. Participants do not receive a salary but are treated as a full-time employee with their part to play in the success of their host business.

EDUCATION

Address	101 Lorna Road
	Hove
	East Sussex BN3 3EL
Telephone	01273 220261
Fax	01273 220376

EDUCATION

COUNCIL ON INTERNATIONAL EDUCATIONAL EXCHANGE (CIEE)

Provides international work and study programmes in over 20 countries

If you are looking to broaden your horizons, gain international experience and have a great time abroad, you could take advantage of the international work and study opportunities available through the Council on International Educational Exchange. Council UK offers more than 50 work and study programmes in 28 countries worldwide. Programmes last from a week to 18 months and are open to students – from high school through to graduate level – and professionals. Work Abroad opportunities include: career and study related work programmes in the USA and Canada – for students (18+), recent graduates and professionals; a work and travel programme in Australia – for 18-25 year olds; teaching opportunities in Japan and China – for graduates, including current and recently retired teachers. Study Abroad options include language study abroad – with study locations in France, Germany, Italy, China, Brazil, Chile, Mexico, Russia and Spain. Most programmes are open to gap-year students and above – some available for 16+; summer study in the USA – at UC Berkeley and UCLA in California and Johns Hopkins University on the East Coast; study programmes at Council Study Centres around the world; summer camps in the USA – for 10- to 20-year-olds.

Address   52 Poland Street
                   London W1V 4JQ
Telephone   0171 478 2000
Fax   0171 734 7322
E-mail
infouk@ciee.org
Web site
http://www.ciee.org/

CWC ENTERPRISES

Provides training for young people in Central London

The Network (London version of Youth Credits) Training programmes provided by CWC Enterprises combine college study and practical work experience leading to nationally-recognised qualifications. Most trainees on a Network Programme are given a weekly training allowance, this is £29.50 at age 16 and £35 at age 17 and over. They also get help with their travel expenses. Some trainees are employed by the organisation which provides their work-experience, and are paid a wage by their employer. Courses available are in Film and Television Lighting, Photography, Initial Training – English for

EDUCATION

speakers of other languages, Gas Apprentices, Graphics, Engineering Technicians, Sport and Recreation, Video and Media. Applications available from March. Phone or write for an application form. Applications are accepted until programmes are full. Interviews take place at the end of March, courses beginning in September.

Address   c/o Training Services
City of Westminster College
Ladbroke Grove Centre
Lancaster Road W11 1QT
Telephone   0171 258 2888
Fax   0171 258 2986

DRAGONS INTERNATIONAL

Dragons International is a commercial company specialising in exchange holidays to France and Germany. They can also offer escorted travel to France for those who already have an exchange partner or host family and simply need to travel there and back. Applicants for exchanges are matched with a partner of similar age, interests and background and the exchanges take place at various times between April and September. Supervised travel is provided throughout the journey to France and passengers are collected from 16 different meeting points in the UK.

Costs/waiting lists

The cost depends on the UK point of departure and varies from about £150 to £200. This includes the return fare, supervised travel, matching of partners and insurance. Early application is recommended as applications are dealt with as received

Address   Godswell House
                    Bloxham
                    Banbury
                    Oxon OX15 4ES
Telephone   01295 721717
Fax   01295 721991

EN FAMILLE OVERSEAS (EFO)

Arrange paying-guest stays with host families in France, Spain, Italy and Germany

EFO offers you the chance to get to know a foreign country and its people, to speak the language, and experience family life by arranging for you to stay with a host family, mainly in France but also in Germany, Italy and Spain. You will be treated as one of the family, taking part in all the family activities and meeting their friends and relations, making it an ideal way to improve your spoken language and make new friends. Special language holidays are also available which provide some form of tuition, ranging from classes at a language school through to

EDUCATION

intensive language practice whilst staying with a teacher's family.

How to contact
Telephone or SAE for advice and information
Costs/waiting lists
Fees are approx £55. Host family weekly charges in European countries approx £185-£270. Language courses cost from £545 for two weeks including accommodation and lessons. No waiting lists but six weeks' notice of stay is preferred

Address	The Old Stables
	60b Maltravers Street
	Arundel
	West Sussex BN18 9BG
Telephone	01903 883266
Fax	01903 883582

ENGLISH SPEAKING UNION (ESU)

Provides educational programmes and scholarships for exchanges

The ESU organises the Secondary School Exchange scholarship programme for young people who wish to spend a gap year studying at an American or Canadian high school between A-levels and university. Scholarships to study in the US are also offered in music, library science, physical sciences and teaching. The ESU also offers international exchanges for students and young professionals in the fields of law, medicine, agriculture, finance and current affairs. ESU promotes international public speaking, mooting and debating with various competitions. Finally, ESU offers English conversational classes to foreign students and young professionals working in London via the English in Action programme.

Address	Dartmouth House
	37 Charles Street
	Mayfair
	London W1X 8AB
Telephone	0171 493 3328
Fax	0171 495 6108
E-mail	

esu@mailbox.ulcc.ac.uk

EURO-ACADEMY

Learn the language on location. Home stays and language courses in France, Austria, Germany, Spain, Italy and Portugal all year round for all levels and ages. Ideal for those about to take GCSEs or A-levels, gap-year students and undergraduates. Also available are vacation courses with leisure activities and sports options (tennis, riding, windsurfing etc) with drawing and painting in Italy.

EDUCATION

EDUCATION

Numbers passing through
c.500 individuals and 300 travelling in groups
Costs/waiting lists
Home stays cost from £210 (one week) to £385 (two weeks). Vacation courses from £605 to £890 (two weeks). French university summer schools from £580 (three weeks) to £945. Full details in Euro-Academy brochure. Travel grants for approved study visits are available from LEAs – apply through school or college. Information on scholarships for long term study abroad can be obtained from the cultural section of the relevant embassy. Bookings should ideally be made 2-3 months in advance but can be accepted later within one month

Address	77A George Street
	Croydon
	Surrey CR0 1LD
Telephone	0181 686 2363
Fax	0181 681 8850

EXPERIMENT IN INTERNATIONAL LIVING

Provides educational and cultural exchanges

EIL is a non-profit-making, non-political and non-religious organisation, existing to promote international understanding, and has been involved in international education and exchange since 1932, working mainly through the 'home stay' principle, sending and receiving people to and from more than 50 countries worldwide, either in groups or as individuals. As well as its main programme of individual home stays, EIL can arrange youth exchanges, including Young Worker and Disabled and Disadvantaged programmes with EU and East European countries, Language Acquisition programmes in many countries and much more. They can also arrange a one-year Au Pair Home Stay programme to the USA.

Costs/waiting lists
Costs vary enormously depending on the type of programme, the country visited and the length of stay. Language courses tend to cost more. Eight weeks' notice before departure is required. Write or telephone for a comprehensive brochure with full information

Address	287 Worcester Road
	Malvern
	Worcestershire WR14 1AB
Telephone	01684 562577
Fax	01684 562212

EDUCATION

EDUCATION

FULBRIGHT COMMISSION (US-UK EDUCATIONAL COMMISSION)

The Fulbright Educational Advisory Service

The Fulbright Commission's Educational Advisory Service provides information and advice on all aspects of the US education system and study in the United States. They have a resource centre, reference library and computer centre. They also have educational advisers who can answer questions and provide advice about US education at all levels. Events are held throughout the year for those interested in undergraduate, postgraduate or university exchange study in the USA.

How to contact
For further information send an A4 stamped addressed envelope or go to the Commission itself. Remember to specify the area and level of study

Eligibility
UK citizen holding or expecting to obtain minimum 2:1 honours degree. Awards are available to fund one year of study at postgraduate level in the US in any field, preference is given to people who have graduated in the last five years

Address	62 Doughty Street
	London WC1N 2LS
Telephone	0171 404 6994
Fax	0171 404 6874

E-mail
education@fulbright.co.uk
Web site
http://www.fulbright.co.uk

JOHN HALL PRE-UNIVERSITY INTERIM COURSE

Gap year history of art, architecture, music, art, photography courses in Italy

The pre-university interim course has been running for over 30 years. It lasts about seven weeks running from late January to mid March. It is about European Civilisation including History of Art, Architecture and Music. The course begins with an introduction in London, and thereafter in Venice, with optional extensions in Florence (including art classes and a visit to a Renaissance villa and garden) and Rome (including a private visit to Vatican Museums, Raphael's Stanze and Sistine Chapel and Villa D'Este at Tivoli). The course is for students who have just left school – the average age is 18. It is open to Arts and Science students alike. No previous knowledge of European art or music history is required. It offers a foretaste of a university

EDUCATION

style of learning and living. The course is a programme of lectures, classes, walkabouts and special study visits, language teaching, photography, drawing and painting classes and free time and individual visits.

Costs/waiting lists
c.£3,985 including travel to Italy, accommodation, breakfast, dinner, all lectures, art and photography classes, some art materials and photography developing costs, visits to Ravenna, Padova and Palladian Villas. Scholarships offered by the National Association of Decorative and Fine Arts Societies (NADFAS), but only to applicants who have been members of Young NADFAS for at least two consecutive years and who are under 19 at the time of application

Address	12 Gainsborough Road
	Ipswich
	Suffolk IP4 2UR
Telephone	01473 251223
Fax	01473 288009

LAURA ASHLEY FOUNDATION

Provides funds for further education courses

The Laura Ashley Foundation will consider applications for course fees and high travel costs in cases of hardship for any course held at a further education college, eg City and

Guilds, foundation courses, nursery nursing, A-level, GCSE or BTEC.

How to contact
Send a letter explaining what course you want to do including its costs and you will be sent an application form
Costs/waiting lists
Apply before the course begins
Address   2 Cromwell Place
                    London SW7 2JE
Web site
http://www.users.dircon.co.uk/~laf/

NATIONAL EXTENSION COLLEGE (NEC)

Opportunity to study GCSEs, leisure, business and degrees from home

The NEC provides full tuition and resources so that you can study from home. They have a wide range of courses ranging from GCSE level to degrees. They also have business, writing and leisure courses available.

Address   18 Brooklands Avenue
                    Cambridge CB2 2HN
Telephone   01223 316644
Fax   01223 313586
E-mail
nec@dial.pipex.com
Web site
http://www.nec.ac.uk

EDUCATION

NORMAN HART MEMORIAL FUND

The Norman Hart Memorial Fund offers grants for young people undertaking work or study projects in European countries. A limited number of grants to cover travel and related costs are offered each year to supplement finance from other sources, or as initial funding for applicants seeking further support elsewhere. Awards are made to young people of UK nationality and residence who plan short periods of study or work on projects that further the aims of European unification. Particular stress is placed on the individual initiative shown by the applicants. The projects can be in the political, economic, social, cultural, professional, vocational, industrial or commercial fields and applicants, if awarded a grant, are asked to report to the trustees at the end of their projects.

Numbers passing through
Nine grants totalling £3,000 made in 1991
How to contact
By letter only to the Secretary of the Trust for a leaflet, explanatory notes and an application form
Costs/waiting lists
Applications may be made at any time of the year though submission in the early months is recommended. Applications for grants for

projects to be undertaken during the summer months should be submitted by 31 May at the latest

Address	European Movement
	Dean Bradley House
	52 Horseferry Road
	London SW1P 2AF
Telephone	0171 233 1422
Fax	0171 799 2817

OPEN UNIVERSITY

Offers further education to adults

For those unable to continue their education after age 18, the Open University offers supported distance learning in most academic subjects. It also offers career-linked courses in Management Studies, Computers/Computing in Commerce and Industry and Manufacturing Management Techniques. These can lead to an MBA (recognised by AMBA) and an MBA-Technology. Courses for those in education and those in health and social welfare. There is also a leisure series for various interests and hobbies.

Address	Walton Hall
	Milton Keynes MK7 6AA
Telephone	01908 653 231

EDUCATION

PEOPLE FIRST

Learning difficulties

Self-help group of people with learning difficulties who meet together in groups for self advocacy. The London office is an information exchange for local groups and others around the country. Newsletter and other publications.

Groups served
People with learning difficulties

Address	Instrument House
	207-215 Kings Cross Road
	London WC1X 9DB
Telephone	0171 713 6400
Fax	0171 833 1880

SHELL TECHNOLOGY ENTERPRISE PROGRAMME (STEP)

Provides work placements for second year undergraduates during summer holidays

STEP aims to link small businesses and undergraduates to their mutual benefit. Selected university students take on placements with small firms for eight weeks during the summer vacation. They tackle a specific business development project as identified by the host manager. The scheme gives students an insight into how business works and the opportunity to learn about teamwork, problem-solving, communication and decision-making. Students make presentations on their projects at the end of the placement and compete for awards. The experience contributes to CVs and provides valuable references.

How to contact
The best way to contact is through one of the 80 agencies around the UK which manage the programme locally or ask at your Careers Office for an application form in the spring. A full list of agencies is available from the above address

Costs/waiting lists
No costs. Students receive a weekly training allowance of £100 for the eight weeks

Address   11 St Bride Street
                  London EC4A 4AS
Telephone   0171 936 3556
Fax   0171 936 3531
E-mail
101776,3176@compuserve/com
Web site
http://biz.ukonline.co.uk/step

EDUCATION

SOCRATES

Education exchange for all levels of education

Objectives: Socrates wants to develop the European dimension in education at all levels so as to strengthen the spirit of European citizenship, drawing on the cultural heritage of each member state; it wants to promote a quantitative and qualitative improvement of knowledge of the languages of the European Union; they want to promote the intercultural dimension of education; it encourages mobility for students, enabling them to complete part of their studies in another member state.

Address	UK Socrates-Erasmus Student Grants Council Research and Development Building University of Kent Canterbury CT2 7PD
Telephone	01227 762712
Fax	01227 762711

STUDENT LOANS COMPANY LTD

Provides loans to students

The Student Loans Company (SLC) lends money to students at a rate of interest equal to that of inflation (currently 2.7% per annum). All eligible students can borrow money from SLC, up to the maximum set by the government each year. Students apply for the loan by filling in an eligibility form and questionnaire at college/university, or a re-application form which is sent to their home. Borrowers begin to repay their loan in the April after they have finished or otherwise left their courses unless their gross income is less than 85% of national average earnings (currently £1316 per month gross) in which case they can apply to defer payment for up to a year at a time.

Address	100 Bothwell Street
	Glasgow G2 7JD
Telephone	0141 306 5000
Fax	0141 306 2005
Web site	

http://www.slc.co.uk

EDUCATION

TRANS-EUROPEAN MOBILITY PROGRAMME
FOR UNIVERSITY STUDIES (TEMPUS)

TEMPUS offers financial support for joint European projects which link enterprises and/or universities in central or Eastern European countries with partners in at least two EC countries. It gives mobility grants for HE staff and students and support for youth exchanges. Applications may involve Albania, the Baltic states, Bulgaria, Croatia, the Czech and Slovak states, Hungary, Poland, Romania and Slovenia. Contact the above address for more details.

Address   Research and Development
                 Building
                 University of Kent
                 Canterbury CT2 7PD
Telephone   01227 824067
Fax   01227 823468
E-mail
tempusuk@ukc.ac.uk

UCAS – UNIVERSITIES AND COLLEGES
ADMISSIONS SERVICE

Processes applications to all UK universities

Also processes applications to most colleges of higher education.

Numbers passing through

In excess of 400,000 applicants. Telephone or send a letter to enquiries. It is best to apply early. The deadline date for receipt of application forms is 15 December (15 October for those applying to Oxford or Cambridge) of the year preceding entry. Handbooks and forms are available free of charge from schools, colleges and careers offices. Instructions on how to apply are contained within the form. The application fee is £12, or £4 if applying to one course or institution

Address	Fulton House
	Jessop Avenue
	Cheltenham
	Gloucestershire GL50 3SH
Telephone	01242 227788
Fax	01242 221622

E-mail
enq@ucas.ac.uk
Web site
http://www.ucas.ac.uk

EDUCATION

UK COURSE DISCOVERER

Searchable database of all the courses available throughout the UK

Produced by ECCTIS 2000 Ltd, UK Course Discoverer, ECCTIS+ is a government-owned, computerised course service giving information on over 100,000 courses in all universities and colleges of further and higher education. It is available at over 5,500 access points throughout the UK, in schools, further and higher education colleges, careers offices, libraries, TECs and LECs. UK Course Discoverer is available by subscription on compact disc with up to six updates per year. Whatever your starting point and interest you can find information on a course for you. You can search by any combination of subject, method of study, type of study and geographical area to find who offers courses in your chosen subject area. You can read about entry requirements, course outline and content as well as institutional details. During August and September, ECCTIS 2000 also provides a vacancy information service for degree and HND courses. Whether it is a degree, postgraduate, further edcuation, vocational, access or professional course you need, UK Course Discover can help provide the answer.

Address   Oriel House
       Oriel Road
       Cheltenham
       Gloucester GL50 1XP
Telephone 01242 252627
Fax   01242 258600
E-mail
101472.2254@compuserve
Web site
http://www.ecctis.co.uk

EDUCATION

PUBLICATIONS

AWARDS FOR FIRST DEGREE STUDY AT COMMONWEALTH UNIVERSITIES 1995-1997

A guide to over 160 schemes of scholarships, bursaries, grants, loans etc for Commonwealth students wishing to study for a first degree at university in another Commonwealth country. Many of the awards are for students from developing countries and a substantial number are open to students of any nationality.

Publisher	Association of Commonwealth Universities Awards 36 Gordon Square London WC1H 0PS
Telephone	0171 387 8572
Fax	0171 387 2655
Price	£10.00
ISBN	0 85143 159 3

AWARDS FOR POSTGRADUATE STUDY AT COMMONWEALTH UNIVERSITIES 1995-1997

Comprises 1,070 entries describing scholarships, grants, bursaries, loans etc for graduates of Commonwealth universities for postgraduate study or research at a

EDUCATION

Commonwealth university outside their own country. An international directory with over 600 awards open to students of any nationality and over 250 tenable in any country.

Publisher	Association of Commonwealth Universities Awards
	36 Gordon Square
	London WC1H 0PS
Telephone	0171 387 8572
Fax	0171 387 2655
Price	£24.00
ISBN	0 85143 158 5

EDUCATION YEARBOOK 96/97, THE

Comprehensive guide to all areas of education

The *Education Yearbook* is published annually and provides information on all aspects of education. It covers higher, further and vocational education including universities and colleges, business, technical and mangement education, art and design, music, dance and drama colleges and independent further education establishments. The employment and careers section contains details of Industrial Training Boards, the careers services, professional

EDUCATION

bodies and sponsored training and apprenticeships. Studying and travelling abroad are widely covered from details of exchange visits, voluntary service and working holidays to European organisations, European schools, the British Council and embassies and institutes providing further information on education and travel abroad. You can usually find this book in your local library or school.

Price £85.00
ISBN 0 27362 761 9

EDUCATIONAL GRANTS DIRECTORY, THE

A list of educational charities

The most comprehensive listing of educational charities which support children and students in need up to first degree level. This publication covers over 260 national and general sources of help, giving a total of £32 million a year in educational grants to individuals.

Price £16.95

GAP YEAR GUIDEBOOK, THE

For loads of information on planning your gap year

Published each year when A-level results come out, this guide is packed with facts and anecdotes for those who want to take a year off between A-level and university. The book is best read by sixth formers before they fill out their university entrance forms. It takes you through UCAS and form-filling and A-level retake procedures. It covers office skills and other training courses for gap-year jobs and gives gap-year opportunities at Britain's biggest companies as well as pointing out organised work experience schemes. Overseas voluntary work organisations are included and their placements overseas are listed under country headings. There are travel tips and details of language courses and feedback from students runs right through the book. The book can be bought in most bookshops or bought directly from the publishers, Peridot Press (additional £1 for p&p).

Address	2 Blenheim Crescent
	London W11 1NN
Telephone	0171 221 7404
Fax	0171 792 0833

EDUCATION

E-mail
peridot@atlas.co.uk
Web site
http://www.peridot.co.uk
Price £7.95
ISBN 0 95197 559 2

GUIDE TO COURSES & CAREERS IN ART, CRAFT & DESIGN

Clearly designed reader-friendly publication is researched to meet all needs for students as well as teachers. Also includes information on new Universities and Colleges Admissions Service (UCAS) procedures which commence in 1997. Special emphasis is given on how to negotiate the 'from school to college' hurdle.

Available from: NSEAD
The Gatehouse
Corsham Court
Corsham
Wilts, SN13 0BZ
Price £12.30
ISBN 0 90468 422 9

EDUCATION

MEDIA COURSES UK 1997

Media Courses UK gives practical advice and up-to-date information on media courses available throughout the United Kingdom, including what topics are covered in the syllabus, what qualifications are needed for entry, the length of the course, the proportions of practical and academic work, whether the course is specialised or covers several different media, whether it combines media with other subjects and what qualifications the course will lead to. Essential reading for students, parents and careers officers, this book is an important guide for making the right career decision. Price £8.99 from bookshops etc, or £9.99 (inc. p&p) from BFI Publishing, 21 Stephen Street, London, W1P 2LN

Price   £8.99

MULTI-MEDIA: A LISTING OF SHORT COURSES

Courses in Film, Television, Video and Radio

This booklet gives details of short courses in the fields of film, television, video and radio across the UK. Updated three times a year, course titles, duration, entry requirements, institute addresses, phone numbers and costs. Reliable and comprehensive. This publication is not available from bookshops.

From: Plymbridge Distribution Ltd
Estover Road
Plymouth, PL6 7PZ
Telephone 01752 202 301
Price £2.50 plus p&p (50p second class, £1.13 first class)
ISBN 0 85170 587 1

POSTGRADUATE AWARDS

A guide on government awards to postgraduate students

This guide tells you whether you are eligible for the various grants and bursaries available and how to apply for them. It also has a list of other organisations that provide funding for postgraduate courses. Contact the Department of Education and Employment for a copy.

Price Free
ISBN 0 85522 464 9

PUSH GUIDE TO WHICH UNIVERSITY 97, THE

Comprehensive guide to choosing your university

The Push Guide to Which University is a great help if you are trying to choose where you want to go for your degree. Apart from the obvious help – like which universities do which courses, this guide gives you the low down on everything. Whether it's the male/female ratio, clubs and entertainment you are worried about or accommodation and welfare services – this guide has it.

Other useful information includes chapters on student finance, taking a year out and students with disabilities.

EDUCATION

How to contact
To order your copy write/fax or phone Customer Services, McGraw-Hill Publishing Company, Shoppenhamgers Road, Maidenhead, Berkshire SL6 2QL
Telephone   01628 23432
Fax   01628 35895
Web site
http//www.mcgraw-hill.co.uk/push
Price   £9.95
ISBN   0 07709 313 5

SPORTS SCHOLARSHIPS & COLLEGE ATHLETIC PROGRAMS IN THE USA

College-by-college guide to sports scholarships in the USA

American colleges possess some of the best facilities in the world for developing the sporting abilities of their students; they also offer thousands of sports scholarships worth millions of dollars to attract men and women with talent from all over the world. This book gives a college-by-college guide to sports scholarships and collegiate sports programmes for men and women who would like to use their athletic abilities to help pay their college bills while they study in the US, or to improve their chances of admission to a US college. In the past foreigners have rarely taken up these scholarships because they lacked the information necessary to get them – this book explains how to go about it.

Address	Vacation Work Publications
	9 Park End Street
	Oxford OX1 1HU
Telephone	01865 241 978
Fax	01865 790 885
Price	£12.99
ISBN	1 56079 234 5

EDUCATION

STUDENT GRANTS AND LOANS

Information on how to apply for grants and loans

This is a guide explaining the ins and outs of applying for government grant and loan schemes as a student. It covers the types you can get, whether you would be eligible or not, how to apply and how paying back the loan works. You can get a copy from the Department of Education and Employment.

Price	Free
ISBN	0 85522 482 7

EDUCATION

INFORMATION

ASSOCIATION OF GRADUATE CAREERS ADVISORY SERVICES MUTUAL AID SCHEME

This is an agreement amongst careers services in higher education whereby, for the first three years after graduation, you can usually use a nearby careers service if you find it difficult to get to the careers service of the institution from which you graduated. Under Mutual Aid you can normally use the information room at another careers service, and it may be possible to have a short discussion with a duty advisor. Before visiting a careers service it is suggested that you make contact by telephone or letter to establish the extent of the assistance that you can expect and the opening times.

Graduate Careers Information Booklets
This series of 56 booklets, written by higher education careers staff, provides essential information on careers entered by graduates. As well as providing details of what work is done the booklets give information on how to get professional qualifications, the types of organisations that are offering jobs in the area, statistics, sources of other information etc. The series also contains titles covering general areas such as applications and interviews, using languages, working in Europe – first

steps, alternative work styles. Booklets are available to undergraduates, free of charge, at their campus careers service. Copies can be purchased at £2.35 each (inc post and packing) from CSU, Crawford House, Precinct Centre, Manchester M13 9EP. Details of titles and order form from this address.

NATIONAL PROFICIENCY TEST – VOCATIONAL FOUNDATION CERTIFICATES

Vocational Foundation Certificate aimed at people with learning difficulties

The Vocational Foundation Certificate Scheme (VFCS) provides awards below NVQ Level 1.   Currently courses are available in agriculture, animal care, conservation, construction, employment, floristry, horse care, horticulture, hotel and catering, independent living, information technology, numeracy, literacy and communication, office and reception, pottery, poultry and game keeping, retail, vehicle maintenance and workshop practice. Trainees taking these courses will have any learning difficulties taken into account when being assessed. Certificates are awarded for all elements passed, not just on completion of a range of elements, promoting 'confidence though competence'. The pick-and-mix style of

EDUCATION

course modules means that trainees can choose the elements which they are most likely to be competent in and achieve higher by specialising. Many trainees go on from VFCS to NVQs, but the VFCS is designed as an award in its own right acting as proof of competence and giving confidence to both trainees and employers.

Address   Vocational Foundation
              Certificate Scheme
              National Proficiency Tests
              Council
              Avenue J
              National Agricultural Centre
              Stoneleigh
              Kenilworth
              CV8 2LG
Telephone 01203 696 553
Fax   01203 696 128

EDUCATION

WEB SITES

BRITISH COUNCIL EDUCATION AND TRAINING

Summary of British qualifications

Web site
http://www.britcoun.org/education/resource/insquali.htm

BRITISH COUNCIL – HOW DOES THE EDUCATION SYSTEM WORK?

What qualifications can you obtain? Do you have the right qualifications? List of institutes

Web site
http://www.britcoun.org/eis/britsyst.htm

BRITISH COUNCIL – MEDICAL QUALIFICATIONS

Information on medical qualifications

Web site
http://www.britcoun.org/health/infoshee/hlt7.htm

EDUCATION

BRITISH COUNCIL – QUALIFICATIONS FOR LAW

Qualifications for law/barristers/solicitors etc

Web site
http://www.britcoun.org/governance/proqual.htm

BRITISH COUNCIL – QUALIFICATIONS FOR LAW IN SCOTLAND

Qualifications for law/barristers/solicitors etc in Scotland

Web site
http://www.britcoun.org/governance/proqual3.htm

BRITISH COUNCIL – SCHOOL LEVEL EXAMINATIONS

Information on pre A-level (school level) examinations

Web site
http://www.britcoun.org/education/resource/insexam.htm

COURSE NET

Covers clearing vacancies, choosing a university and postgraduate vacancies

Web site
http://www.hobsons.com

FE COLLEGE LINKS

Hot links to FE colleges around the UK

Web site
http://www.scit.wlv.ac.uk/ukinfo/uk.map.colls
.html

ON-COURSE

Complete listing of every course offered in London, from computers to cooking

Web site
http://www.uk-courses.co.uk

POSTGRADUATE STUDY

What is postgraduate study and how do I apply?

Web site
http://www.open.gov.uk/bc/eis/gradstud.htm

EDUCATION

STUDENT OUTLOOK

General information site for students linking to entertainment, news and help

Web site
http://www.pro-net.co.uk/student

UNIVERSITY LINKS

Hot links to every university in the country

Web site
http://www.scit.wlv.ac.uk:80/ukinfo/
uk.map.html

EDUCATION

FREETIME

ADVENTURE & SPORT

ORGANISATIONS

BACKPACKERS CLUB

Club for lightweight campers

The Backpackers Club provides its members with a comprehensive advisory and information service on all aspects of backpacking. Experienced members are available to assist in selecting the right equipment. The organisation supports and promotes backpacking, whether you are a walker, cyclist, canoeist, or just interested in this way of life. Although they do provide a foreign and overseas travel information service, this information is for lightweight campers as opposed to people travelling around the world cheaply, carrying their belongings in a rucksack. Membership of the club also offers access to a postal lending library, a farm pitch directory, a long distance path site and pitch directory, the club magazine, a special camping equipment and personal effects insurance scheme, the Backpacking Advisory Service, and the opportunity to take part in regular backpacking weekends in various parts of the UK.

FREETIME

Costs/waiting lists
Membership up to 18 years and OAPs: £7 per year. 18+: £12 per year

Address	49 Lyndhurst Road
	Exmouth
	Devon EX8 3DS
Telephone	01395 265 159
Web site	

http://www.catan.demon.co.uk/backpack

BRITISH RED CROSS ACTIVENTURE

Young people are invited to act as companions to children with disabilities and special needs during their adventure holidays which are held at Hindleap Warren Activity Centre in the Ashdown Forest, East Sussex. British Red Cross Activenture hold six one-week holidays a year and our helpers and staff give care and friendship to the young guests who have a variety of disabilities – all under Red Cross supervision. The young people who attend gain knowledge and self-confidence with a new ability to relate to young people less fortunate than themselves.

Address	British Red Cross Sussex Branch
	3 Howard Terrace
	Brighton BN1 3TR
Telephone	01273 737514
Fax	01273 778992

CAMPING CLUB YOUTH (CCY)

Camping Club Youth aims to help and encourage young people to camp in the correct and safest way through instructional weekends as well as 'Fun and Adventure Weekends' enabling them to pass the CCY test. Each member receives *The Fundamentals of Good Camping* handbook, written and published by the club.

Costs/waiting lists
£3 annual subscription

Address	Greenfields House
	Westwood Way
	Coventry CV4 8JH
Telephone	01203 694995
Fax	01203 694886

CAMPING FOR THE DISABLED (CFD)

CFD can give advice and information about equipment, camping sites in the UK and abroad with special facilities and other sources of help for individuals and groups.

Costs/waiting lists
Subscription is £2.50 per year for individuals and £4 for a group

Address	Unit 2a
	Atcham Estate
	Shrewsbury SY4 4UG

FREETIME

| **Telephone** | 01743 761 889 |
| **Fax** | 01743 761 149 |

CYCLISTS' TOURING CLUB (CTC)

The CTC is the governing body for recreational and utility cycling. It is the largest (and oldest – established in 1878) association for cyclists in the UK. Although primarily a membership organisation, the CTC does much work for all cyclists, whatever their age or ability. Cycling is an economical form of transport, it's healthy and it's fun. The CTC organises various events and operates through a large network of local groups with various special interest sections (young people, disabled etc). There are volunteering opportunities in setting up and running local CTC clubs.

Address	Cotterell House
	69 Meadrow
	Godalming
	Surrey GU7 3HS
Telephone	01483 417217
Fax	01483 426994

FREETIME

ENDEAVOUR TRAINING

Runs outdoor activities, community projects and expeditions at home and abroad

Endeavour runs about ten activity weekends a year. Most members are in their late teens or early twenties. Some are much older and this gives it a family feel. They also do things for other people like run summer camps for less privileged children. They organise canoeing, caving and climbing sessions and most years have expeditions in the UK, Europe or further afield.

Costs/waiting lists
Membership fees: £3.50 unwaged; £7.50 employed; £10 family membership. All activities are subsidised to take into account personal circumstances. Most of the work undertaken is funded by the Endeavour Association. Endeavour is a National Educational Charity

Address	Sheepbridge Centre
	Sheepbridge Lane
	Chesterfield S41 9RX
Telephone	01246 454957
Fax	01246 261865
E-mail	

richardalexander@compuserve.com

ENGLISH SPORTS COUNCIL

Provides national and local information on sports

The English Sports Council Information Service provides contact addresses and information on all aspects of sport. Details of career opportunities and courses are available on receipt of a cheque/PO for £2.50.

Regional addresses
Ten regional offices – addresses available from Head Office

Address	16 Upper Woburn Place
	London WC1H 0QP
Telephone	0171 273 1500
Fax	0171 383 5740

FAIRBRIDGE

Offers outdoor activity courses and personal support to unwaged 14-25 year olds

Fairbridge has ten centres across the UK. If you are aged between 14 and 25 and are unwaged, they can offer you the chance to discover new experiences from canoeing to rock climbing, orienteering to abseiling. Most centres run a drop-in-and-all offer of the Fairbridge programme, which is in three parts.

FREETIME

Induction – chance to meet the staff and try out some of the activities which are part of the basic course.

Basic – A group of up to 12 young people go on a 7- to 8-day outdoor activity course including a few days away from the city.

Follow-on – Staff have time to listen to your ideas and discuss them with you, so you can take control of your life. You will get the chance to do more outdoor activity courses, including a three-week course in Scotland or sailing on Fairbridge's Tall Ship, the chance to learn new skills such as first aid, food hygiene or assertiveness and help to find out about local education, training, volunteering and work opportunities.

Address	1 Westminster Bridge Road
	London SE1 7PL
Telephone	0171 928 1704
Fax	0171 928 6016

FRIENDS FOR YOUNG DEAF PEOPLE (FYD)

Organises projects and courses for deaf, hard of hearing and hearing young people

FYD organises an annual programme of projects and courses for deaf, hard of hearing and hearing young people. The intention is to encourage the personal development of individuals, to create opportunities for deaf children and young people to have fun and try out new experiences, and to help integrate deaf and hearing children and young people. Recent projects include conservation holidays, activity weekends, yachting weekends, participating in sports festivals, and adventure weeks. FYD also offers training in leadership skills, fundraising, many types of work experience, and in a number of other areas. Volunteers are always welcome to help out with the work of FYD.

Costs/waiting lists

Costs for courses/projects/training vary. Some help may be available (further details from FYD)

Address	East Court Mansion Council Offices
	College Lane
	East Grinstead
	West Sussex RH19 3LT
Telephone	01342 323444
Fax	01342 410232

JUBILEE SAILING TRUST (JST)

Opportunity to go Tall Ship Sailing

Jubilee Sailing Trust offers people aged 16 to 70+ the opportunity to experience the challenge and adventure of crewing a 490-ton tall ship at sea for up to ten days regardless of their physical ability. Voyages comprise of an equal number of physically disabled and able-bodied people.

Age range
16-70+
How to contact
Telephone or letter (with SAE) to the Voyage Department
Costs/waiting lists
UK voyages range from £270 (4 days) to £670 (10 days); Canaries voyages from £400 (8 days) to £695 (23 days). Associate membership is £15 per year. There are various bursaries and Trusts from which some funding is available – details from JST. Applications should be made two months in advance

Address	Jubilee Yard
	Merlin Quay
	Hazel Road
	Woolston, Southampton
	SO19 7GB
Telephone	01703 449 108
Fax	01703 449 145

E-mail
jst@jst.org.uk
Web site
http://www.jst.org.uk

NATIONAL CAVING ASSOCIATION

Provides information on caving

Provides information on caving and how to get involved.

Address
Monomark House
27 Old Gloucester Street
London WC1N 3XX

OCEAN YOUTH CLUB (OYC)

Ocean Youth Club is a national voluntary youth organisation which aims to provide young people, no matter what their circumstances, with the opportunity to experience the challenge and adventure of life at sea. They operate ten ocean-going vessels based around the British Isles for young people aged 12 upwards. No previous sailing experience is required and they provide all the safety equipment, instruction, food and insurance. All you need to be is reasonably fit and able to swim. It's a prime opportunity to meet new friends – you will be involved in everything on board from sailing and navigation to cooking and cleaning, under the watchful eye of a certified skipper and a team of qualified watch leaders. Those who wish to continue sailing with OYC can join our training scheme and progress to

FREETIME

skipper if they wish. You are also encouraged to get involved in the boats' winter refits and attend reunions and parties at the end of the sailing season.

Costs/waiting lists

Voyages cost about £30-£40 a day depending on the time of year. OYC does have a grant scheme but young people are encouraged to raise some funds themselves. Peak season always books up early – telephone for availability. OYC regularly runs voyages for differently abled young people with special needs. All vessels are fitted with audio compasses to assist visually impaired voyagers

Address	The Bus Station
	South Street
	Gosport
	Hampshire PO12 1EP
Telephone	01705 528421
Fax	01705 522069

E-mail
Webmaster@oyc.org.uk
Web site
http://www.oyc.org.uk/

OUTWARD BOUND TRUST

Provides adventurous outdoor courses in Wales, Lake District and Scotland

You can attend adventurous courses at one of their three centres in Wales, the Lake District or Scotland. On an Outward Bound course you can take part in activities such as canoeing, climbing, camping, hill walking and sailing. You can come on a course as an individual or with a group from school, college, youth club or work. You will be able to meet new people, make friends and have great fun.

Costs/waiting lists

The fees for all courses are fully inclusive of all accommodation, specialist equipment, tuition etc. They range from approx £100-£550. Young people between 14 and 24 may qualify for financial help of up to 50% of the cost of a course. Details from the Trust. Courses during the summer months do tend to get filled quickly, so apply early!

Address	Watermillok
	Penrith
	Cumbria CA11 0JL
Telephone	0990 134 227
Fax	01768 486 983
E-mail	

enquiries@outwardbound-uk.org

FREETIME

ROYAL UK LIFE SAVING SOCIETY
(RLSS UK)

If you want to learn to look after yourself – or take care of others – in the water, RLSS have courses for you, ranging from very basic to professional-level qualifications for lifeguards, which can lead to a job in the leisure industry or active membership of a volunteer lifeguard club. Whatever your swimming ability a life-saving course will make you safer in the water. People with special needs welcome.

How to contact
Phone, letter, fax, or in person to Head Office for advice, information, leaflets etc about the work of RLSS UK, and for local contact information

Costs/waiting lists
Membership: £12.50. For those aged 18 and under membership is £5.00. Exam fees range from 75p-£15. Supporters can give donations. No waiting lists, but some programmes only run at particular times of the year

Address	Mountbatten House
	Studley
	Warwickshire B80 7NN
Telephone	01527 853943
Fax	01527 854453

FREETIME

SAIL TRAINING ASSOCIATION (STA SCHOONERS)

Adventure sailing training on board Tall Ships

The aim of the STA is to help young people learn about themselves, their capabilities and awareness of others in an exciting and demanding voyage on the UK's largest sail-training schooners – the 150ft *Sir Winston Churchill* and *Malcolm Miller*. You do not need any previous experience of the sea or sailing, just an awareness that you are undertaking a challenge, both physically and psychologically, that will stand you in good stead for the rest of your life. During your voyage you and 38 other trainees of varying backgrounds will take a large sailing ship across nearly 1,000 miles of unpredictable sea and visit two/three Northern Continental ports. Alternatively, between November and May, *Sir Winston Churchill* sails the exotic waters of the Canaries off the west coast of Africa. You will be part of the ship's company and as such will take an active part in the care and maintenance of the ship as well as watch duties, including look-out, steering, sail-trimming, galley work and ship cleaning. All voyages count towards the Duke of Edinburgh's Award scheme – Gold Award Residential qualification or the scheme's interest section.

FREETIME

Costs/waiting lists

Low season – two weeks £500; high season – £770, inclusive of all food and equipment, raised from own activities. STA volunteer committees around the country hold fundraising events and Head Office can advise on funds and trusts. It is advisable to book as early as possible

Address	2a The Hard
	Portsmouth PO1 3PT
Telephone	01705 832055
Fax	01705 815769

E-mail
tallships@sta.org.uk
Web site
http://www.sta.org.uk/sta

SCOTTISH SPORTS COUNCIL

The Scottish Sports Council provides information on sport in Scotland and initiates opportunities for people to participate in sport at any level of ability.

Costs/waiting lists

There is a charge for some publications although many are free

Address	Caledonia House
	South Gyle
	Edinburgh EH12 9DQ
Telephone	0131 317 7200
Fax	0131 317 7202

FREETIME

SPORTS COUNCIL FOR NORTHERN IRELAND

The aims of the Sports Council are to further sport and physical recreation in Northern Ireland. If you need any general advice or information about a particular sport and how to get involved, the Sports Council will be able either to help or to point you in the right direction.

Age range
Any
Costs/waiting lists
No costs for information
Address　　　　House of Sport
　　　　　　　　　Upper Malone Road
　　　　　　　　　Belfast BT9 5LA
Telephone　　 01232 381222
Fax　　　　　 01232 682757

SPORTS COUNCIL FOR WALES

The Sports Council for Wales can provide you with information on all sports facilities and organisations in Wales.

Address　　　　Sofia Gardens
　　　　　　　　　Cardiff
　　　　　　　　　CF1 9SW
Telephone　　 01222 300500

FREETIME

YOUNG SKIPPERS SCHEME

Provides opportunities to sail a small yacht, learning teamwork and leadership

The purpose of the Young Skippers Scheme is to provide young sailors with an opportunity to develop their leadership, teamwork and communication skills through the responsibility of sailing small yachts with the minimum of 'adult' supervision. Participants work together to plan their week. No formal qualifications necessary, but applicants should have some experience of helming. Cruises running from June to September.

Costs
A seven-day course costs £120, covering running costs

Address	Southampton Institute
	East Park Terrace
	Southampton
	Hants SO14 0YN
Telephone	01703 319787
Fax	01703 319904

E-mail
moat_a@solent.ac.uk

PUBLICATIONS

ADVENTURE HOLIDAYS 1997

Opportunities for adventure in 1997 in over 100 countries

Crammed full of opportunities for those of any age, including windsurfing, canoeing, hang-gliding etc, with more unusual activities ranging from camel trekking in the Sahara to husky sledging in Greenland. Covers opportunities for people of any age, with or without previous experience and includes full information on types of accommodation, instruction provided, prices of the holidays and requirements for equipment needed, etc.

Address	Vacation Work Publications
	9 Park End Street
	Oxford OX1 1HU
Telephone	01865 241 978
Fax	01865 790 885
Price	£6.99
ISBN	1 85458 158 9

FREETIME

WEB SITES

YAHOO'S UK SPORTS WEB DIRECTORY

Web site
http://www.yahoo.co.uk/Regional/Countries/
United_Kingdom/Recreation_and_Sport/Sport

YELL SPORTS DIRECTORY

**From American football to water sports,
listing of great sports sites**

Web site
http://www.yell.co.uk/yell/newweb/sprtslsr/
index.html

ARTS

ORGANISATIONS

BRITISH FEDERATION OF YOUNG CHOIRS (BFYC)

Provides a variety of singing opportunities for young people throughout the UK

The BFYC organises a wide variety of singing activities and choral events – from workshops with 20 singers to major events involving up to 1,000 singers. Whether the style is gospel, classical, jazz, barbershop, improvisation (or other), their aim is to get young people singing and to enjoy singing. The BFYC also provides training for choral conductors and singing leaders and is keen to encourage people who would like to develop their leadership skills. It can advise you about local activities, keep you informed about events in this country and abroad and provide exciting opportunities to sing at large-scale choral events with orchestras and leading conductors.

Costs/waiting lists

Individual membership is £18; choir £35. Participation fees at choral events range from £5 per choir to £3 per head

FREETIME

Address	Devonshire House
	Devonshire Square
	Loughborough LE11 3DW
Telephone	01509 211664
Fax	01509 260630

BRITISH YOUTH OPERA (BYO)

Every summer BYO provides specialist training opportunities for singers, instrumentalists, conductors, assistant designers/directors, stage crew etc. Under expert professional tuition, two operas are rehearsed which are performed in London and on tour. Young people who apply should already be trained to a reasonably high standard (especially singers).

Age range
Singers 22-30, instrumentalists 18-30
How to contact
SAE with covering letter, or telephone for advice, information and leaflets
Costs/waiting lists
Training courses are free of charge and students receive subsistence whilst they are on tour. For rehearsals in London students are expected to pay for their own accommodation, travel and living expenses etc.

Address	South Bank University
	103 Borough Road
	London SE1 0AA
Telephone	0171 815 6090
Fax	0171 815 6094

EUROPEAN UNION YOUTH ORCHESTRA (EUYO)

The orchestra is for musicians from anywhere in the EU aged between 14 and 23

The European Union Youth Orchestra (EUYO) offers two international training courses and tours per year to talented orchestral musicians. Auditions are held each autumn. Applicants must have an EU passport. All travel and accommodation is provided on tour, there are no costs.

Address	6a Pont Street
	London SW1X 9EL
Telephone	0171 235 7671
Fax	0171 235 7370

FREETIME

INTERNATIONAL THEATRE EXCHANGE (ITE)

Arranges exchanges in theatre and performing arts

International Theatre Exchange is the UK

centre of the International Amateur Theatre Association, an organisation whose main aim is to promote cultural exchange in the area of the performing arts and arts education. It organises and conducts international theatre workshops, festivals and theatrical exchange visits, many of which are based around youth and student theatre. All the work of the ITE is carried out by experienced people volunteering their services and funding is provided by 'friends' – individuals and groups involved in theatre in any of its forms, whether student, amateur, professional, school, fringe or community theatre.

How to contact
Write to the address below enclosing SAE

Address   Company Secretary
                 19 Abbey Park Road
                 Great Grimsby
                 North East Lincolnshire
                 DN32 0HJ
Telephone   01472 343424

NATIONAL FEDERATION OF MUSIC SOCIETIES (NFMS)

NFMS is the national body covering all types of music societies. It can put you in touch with a local society or offer help and advice to anyone who wants to set up a new music club or society. Most of its member societies are orchestras and choirs but it is keen to encourage other types of music such as jazz, steel bands, folk music, Indian music etc.

Regional addresses
12 regions – contact through Head Office
Age range
Any
Costs/waiting lists
Costs vary between societies

Address	Francis House
	Francis Street
	London SW1P 1DE
Telephone	0171 828 7320
Fax	0171 828 5504
E-mail	

postmaster@nfms.demon.co.uk

NATIONAL STUDENT DRAMA FESTIVAL (NSDF)

Festival offering training and career opportunities in drama

The NSDF offers major training and career opportunities to students of all ages (though preferably over 15), as well as recreation and training opportunities for everyone, plus sheer enjoyment, outstanding stimulation and useful contacts. The festival itself is seven days, crammed with professionally-led workshops (usually two sessions a day), about

FREETIME

14 selected productions from the whole UK (schools, youth theatres, colleges, drama schools and ad hoc groups), a daily mass discussion of plays seen, and a daily festival newspaper with contributions from anyone. There is a summary by theatre professionals, who give awards to eveything considered outstanding; but the emphasis is on sharing and learning, instead of competition. It takes place just before or just after Easter (next date is 1-8 April 1998) in Scarborough. Some shows transfer to Edinburgh (perhaps with the National Sudent Theatre Company, which also presents new productions, cast nationwide, when finance permits) and/or London.

Address	20 Lansdowne Road
	Muswell Hill
	London N10 2AU
Telephone	0181 883 4586
Fax	0181 883 7142
Web site	

http://www.nsdf.uk.inter.net

POETRY SOCIETY, THE

Encourages, advises readers and writers, runs competitions and workshops

The Society is a membership organisation which encourages young people to read and write poetry. It has an education department which puts poets into schools and produces a range of educational publications. We run workshops for children and young adults and give free advice and information on publishing, competitions, contacts for poets and poetry organisations and much more. We publish two magazines which feature new writing and have a website *The Poetry Place*. We also have a poetry cafe that has a programme of readings and events, as well as exhibitions.

Costs/waiting lists
Membership as a friend £10. Full membership for students £20 (including magazine subscriptions), non-members can also write/ring in for free information

Address	22 Betterton Street
	London WC2H 9BU
Telephone	0171 240 4810
Fax	0171 240 4818

E-mail
poetrysoc@dial.pipex.com
Web site
http://www.poetrysoc.com

FREETIME

TALENT CORPORATION INTERNATIONAL (TCI)

Aims to develop, nurture and promote talent and cultural expressions

TCI helps young people through the provision of training seminars, workshops and cultural industries business development revolving around music. The organisation is a network and has access to a range of facilities including rehearsal and recording studios, video recording facilities and information technology/reprographic resources. It also provides self-development training, self-defence classes and record production services.

Address	53A Craven Park
	Harlesden
	London NW10 8FR
Telephone	0181 961 3558
Fax	0181 961 8400

WEEKEND ARTS COLLEGE (WAC)

Provides art training for 5-25-year-olds from low income families

Weekend Arts College (WAC) provides training in performing arts (music, dance and drama) for young people. Classes take place at the weekend, in the evenings and in school

FREETIME

holidays. WAC places a special emphasis on young people from low income families, and 60% of its students are from black and ethnic minorities. WAC also offers specialist provision for young people with disabilities, many of whom go on to mainstream classes. WAC is particularly committed to enabling young people to develop distinctive voices which represent their own cultural backgrounds.

Costs/waiting lists
There is a fee to take a class but it is no more than £1.50 per class. There is a waiting list for courses and it is advisable to apply as early as possible

Address	Interchange
	Dalby Street
	Kentish Town
	London NW5 3NG
Telephone	0171 284 1861
Fax	0171 482 5292
E-mail	

wac@cerbernet.co.uk

FREETIME

WORLD STUDENT DRAMA TRUST

Funds Annual International Student Playscript competition

The Annual International Student Playscript competition is free to enter. It is judged by

Professor Peter Thomson (Exeter University Drama Department), Stephen Jeffreys (semi-final) and Alan Ayckbourn (final). All entries receive a written criticism and are considered for first performance by the National Student Theatre Company. First prize is £400.

How to contact
Write sending a stamped, self-addressed envelope to the address below (but do not send your scripts)

Address	20 Landsdown Road
	Muswell Hill
	London N10 2AU
Telephone	0181 883 4586
Fax	0181 883 7142

YOUNG CONCERT ARTISTS TRUST (YCAT)

Agency promoting outstanding young soloists and chamber musicians

The YCAT is set up to identify, nurture and promote outstanding young soloists and chamber musicians emerging into the profession at a time when commercial management is not available to them. YCAT artists receive a complete management service for an initial three-year period plus YCAT Presentation Concerts in London and Manchester and opportunities to take part in the presitgious YCAT Wigmore Lunchtime

Series. Auditions are held annually in London. Preliminary auditions take place at the Wigmore Hall in February/March; semi-finals at the Guildhall School of Music in April with a Public Final Audition at the Wigmore Hall early in June. The auditions are open to all instruments but categories vary from year to year. Musicians should be resident in the United Kingdom with permission to work here for at least five years. No set number of artists will be selected. If none meet the standard, none will be selected. If all the finalists meet the standard they will all be offered representation.

Address	23 Garrick Street
	London WC2E 9AX
Telephone	0171 379 8477
Fax	0171 379 8467

YOUTH AND MUSIC

Discounts up to 50% on tickets for arts events

Youth and Music runs a nationwide ticket concessionary scheme, Stage Pass, which can enable you to get up to 50% off tickets to performances at venues around the country, details of which are contained in a monthly magazine sent to all members. Youth and Music is also the British section of the Féderation Internationale des Jeunesses

FREETIME

Musicales and is responsible for the recruitment of British musicians and singers for the Féderation's worldwide activities including the World Orchestra and World Choir. It also promotes its own concerts targeted for young audiences new to music, and is in the process of developing an educational programme.

Costs/waiting lists

Stage Pass costs: £17.50 for London and South East, £10.50 outside this area. Stage Pass entitles you to buy two discounted tickets and provides a monthly events magazine

Address   28 Charing Cross Road
              London WC2H 0DB
Telephone 0171 379 6722
Fax   0171 497 0345
E-mail
stagepass@dial.pipex.com

ORGANISATIONS

BG PLC YOUNG WILDLIFE PHOTOGRAPHER OF THE YEAR COMPETITION

Young Wildlife Photographer of the Year is the junior section of the International Wildlife Photographer of the Year competition, and is open to people aged 17 years and under. The competition is judged in three age categories and all entries must be photographs of wild animals, plants or wild places. The winning entries from the junior and main competition are published in the *BBC Wildlife* magazine and are included in an exhibition at the Natural History Museum, London and on tour around the UK and overseas.

How to contact
Telephone, fax or letter to the below address for application forms available every April, the closing date for entries is mid-May

Address	Natural History Museum
	Cromwell Road
	London SW7 5BD
Telephone	0171 938 8714
Fax	0171 938 8788
E-mail	

WildPhoto@nhm.ac.uk

FREETIME

BP PORTRAIT AWARD

The BP Portrait Award is an annual competition aimed at encouraging young artists to take up portraiture. The competition is judged from original paintings with a first prize of £10,000, a second prize of £4,000 and third prize of £2,000. An exhibition of works selected from the entries is held at the National Portrait Gallery and in the past many artists who have had their work shown have gained commissions as a result.

Numbers passing through
Over 700 entries in 1995
How to contact
Write, with an SAE, for an application form
Costs/waiting lists
£5 registration fee. Closing date for applications is early April

Address	National Portrait Gallery
	St Martin's Place
	London WC2H 0HE
Telephone	0171 306 0055
Fax	0171 306 0056

CHALLENGE TO YOUTH

The BP Challenge to Youth programme comprises a number of schemes and competitions which give you and your friends the opportunity to work as a team to come up

FREETIME

with designs and to build practical objects to the benefit of the community or the environment. The purpose of the Challenges is 'to bridge the gap between the theory of the classroom and the practicality of the adult world'. Cash prizes are awarded for working well as a team, for innovation and for the success of their designs. Current challenges include the 'Buildacar' competition which has proved such a success that it now takes place every two years. Other projects have involved using technology to solve the problems faced by the elderly in their homes, or to design and produce aids for the disabled. Starter packs, advice and other needs are provided throughout the duration of all projects. 'Challenges' change from year to year but they always involve design, technology, making decisions, achieving results and teamwork.

Costs/waiting lists

Write to the address below, through your school or youth group, for details of current competitions

Address	BP Oil UK Ltd
	Community and Educational
	Affairs Department
	BP House
	Breakspear Way
	Hemel Hempstead HP2 4UL
Telephone	01442 225011
Fax	01442 225919

FREETIME

DUKE OF EDINBURGH'S AWARD, THE

Opportunities for personal achievement, adventure and community work for 14-25-year-olds

The Duke of Edinburgh's Award is for all young people, whatever their background or ability, between the ages of 14 and 25. It gives opportunities for personal achievements, adventure, community and social involvement and a widening of interests. There are three levels of Award: Bronze, Silver and Gold. Each requires an increasing degree of commitment. To gain any one of these levels you must complete four sections. Expeditions, Skills, Physical Recreation and Service, plus complete a Residential Project working away from home for at least five days. 58 countries operate the Award and about 25,000 people take part at any one time.

Address	Gulliver House
	Madeira Walk
	Windsor
	Berks SL4 1EU
Telephone	01753 810753
Fax	01753 810666

E-mail
awardhq@dea.sonnet.co.uk
Web site
http://www.sonnet.co.uk/dea

FREETIME

SOCIAL INVENTIONS COMPETITION

The Institute for Social Inventions runs an annual competition, with prizes for both adults and young people, for novel ideas and projects that will improve the quality of life within our society. A social invention is defined as a new and imaginative solution to a social problem – not a product, nor a technological invention, nor a patentable device – but a means by which society can be improved. Good examples of past social inventions include the Forest Garden in Shropshire and Green Miles, collecting mileage points for free public transport – new combinations of existing ideas, new ways for people to relate to each other, new organisational structures or whatever. ISI offer £1,000 a year for the best social invention (entry deadline 1 June every year), and they are editors of *The Book of Visions – An Encyclopaedia of Social Innovations* (price £18.49 inc p&p). They also hold walking groups every Saturday where you can meet the up-and-coming Social Inventors and swap ideas.

Address	The Institute for Social Inventions 20 Heber Road London NW2 6AA
Telephone	0181 208 2853

FREETIME

Fax   0181 452 6434
E-mail
rhino@dial.pipex.com

WHITBREAD YOUNG VOLUNTEER AWARDS

Recognise young volunteers

The Whitbread Volunteer Action Award Scheme is designed to recognise and reward young people who give up their own time for the benefit of others, especially those disadvantaged by disability, sickness, situation or age. There are three categories in the Award, one for individual volunteers and one for volunteering groups, with a prize of £1,000 for each category.

Costs/waiting lists

No costs or waiting lists. The Award Scheme is usually launched in June each year and the winners are announced in November

Address   Freepost (LOL 1936)
                   Luton
                   Bedfordshire LU1 3YR
Telephone   01582 397759
Fax   01582 397757

FREETIME

BOYS' BRIGADE

The Boys' Brigade offers a wide range of social and sporting activities

The Boys' Brigade offers a wide range of social and sporting activities. It offers opportunities for year-round activities, including helping the elderly or the disabled in the community, or participating in award schemes, such as the Duke of Edinburgh's Award, through activities such as camping, canoeing, life-saving, arts and crafts. Camp sites, mountaineering clubs and outdoor centres throughout the UK provide a wealth of exciting opportunities. The Boys' Brigade is a Christian, uniformed organisation.

Address	Felden Lodge
	Felden
	Hemel Hempstead
	Herts HP3 0BL
Telephone	01442 231681
Fax	01442 235391

FREETIME

BRITISH YOUTH COUNCIL (BYC)

The British Youth Council is the representative body for people aged between 16 and 25 in the UK, working to increase the participation of young people at all levels of political and public decision-making. BYC's primary aim is to advance the interests and views of young people and to enable them to play a more active part in decisions that affect their lives. BYC is run by young people. They come together at council meetings to debate and discuss ideas and they elect a Management Committee to carry out policy decisions. All the main voluntary youth organisations are a part of BYC, as are many local youth councils and political youth groups. BYC publishes a wide range of political education materials suitable for young people. In addition, a Youth Information and Briefing service provides subscribers with regular updates on issues affecting young people, including occasional 'in brief' policy papers and quarterly facts and figures sheets. In 1996 BYC organised M-Power, a high-profile young voter registration campaign aimed at increasing young people's representation on the electoral register and encouraging young people to use their vote in the general election.

FREETIME

Address	65-69 White Lion Street
	London N1 9PP
Telephone	0171 278 0582
Fax	0171 383 3545

CAMPHILL VILLAGE TRUST

Regional addresses
The Trust runs village communities in Aberdeen, North Yorkshire, Hertfordshire, Gloucestershire, West Midlands, Cleveland and Dumfries. Full details from Head Office
Age range
Any
Costs/waiting lists
None for advice and information

Address	Delrow House
	Hillfield Lane
	Aldenham
	Watford WD2 8DJ
Telephone	01923 856006
Fax	01923 858035

CHURCH OF ENGLAND YOUTH SERVICES

Provides support, advice, consultancy and training to young people

The Church of England Youth Services promotes the education, spiritual and social development of young people. Support,

FREETIME

advice, consultancy, and training is offered through a wide range of opportunities locally, regionally and nationally. Young adult participation at all levels in the church is encouraged and specific support is given to the Youth Issues Group of the Committee of Minority Ethnic Concerns and the Young Adult Network. Projects and initiatives are often undertaken in partnership and in collaboration with other denominations and Christian youth work agencies.

Address	Board of Education
	Church House
	Great Smith Street
	London SW1P 3NZ
Telephone	0171 222 9011 Ext 408
Fax	0171 233 1094

CRUSADERS

Christian youth group with holidays and volunteering opportunities

In addition to being a Christian youth organisation running youth groups and holidays, it provides a diverse programme of short term service opportunities. Volunteers are given the opportunity to run holiday camps, help on projects with the homeless, work on practical projects in the Third World or join youth work parties. Training is provided in most instances.

FREETIME

Costs/waiting lists

Volunteers are given guidance in raising support and funding assistance is occasionally given

Address	2 Romeland Hill
	St Albans
	Herts AL3 4ET
Telephone	01727 855422
Fax	01727 848518

E-mail
crusaders@ukonline.co.uk

GIRLS VENTURE CORPS AIR CADETS (GVCAC)

Uniformed organisation for girls

The GVCAC offers a wide and challenging range of activities aimed at giving its members a broader outlook and a greater sense of purpose. Activities include camping, canoeing, skiing, rifle-shooting, gliding, drill, drama and handicrafts as well as more unusual pursuits such as theory of aviation and air experience flights in small aircraft. Leadership and initiative training plays a major role and every aspect of the Duke of Edinburgh's Award Scheme is covered.

Costs/waiting lists

Costs include subscriptions, course and camp fees and uniform

FREETIME

Address	Redhill Aerodrome
	Kings Mill Lane
	South Nutfield
	Redhill, Surrey RH1 5JY
Telephone	01737 823345
Fax	01737 823345

GUIDE ASSOCIATION, THE

Opportunity for girls and women to take part in activities and develop skills

Guiding brings together girls and women from all kinds of backgrounds. By working together, they learn to understand each other's needs and respect each other's culture. It offers a chance to explore, to try out a wide variety of games and activities and learn a range of skills, anything from outdoor pursuits, walking, camping, abseiling and canoeing, to working with computers, time management and team building. With worldwide links, there's the opportunity to meet and work with people from other countries, either by travelling abroad or welcoming visitors. The age ranges are Rainbow Guides 5-7 years, Brownie Guides 7-10, Guides 10-15, Ranger Guides 14-25, Young Leaders 14-21.

FREETIME

Address   17-19 Buckingham Palace
                  Road
                  London SW1W 0PT
Telephone   0171 834 6242
Fax   0171 828 8317
E-mail
chq@guides.org.uk
Web site
http://www.guides.org.uk

INTERNATIONAL PEN FRIENDS

Provides an international pen friend service

International correspondence service accepting members from any country in the world. Special sections for stamp collectors, language students etc. Established in 1967.

Address   PO Box 42
                  Berwick Upon Tweed
                  Northumberland TD15 1RU
Telephone/Fax 01289 331335

NATIONAL FEDERATION OF CITY FARMS (NFCF)

Provides volunteer opportunities on city farms and conservation work

NFCF brings the countryside to the city by supporting and advising people who set up

FREETIME

and run small farm holdings in built-up areas where many of us live. It provides volunteering opportunities to work with animals, run play schemes and develop conservation work. The NFCF also provides training, exchanges and looks at ways in which young people can participate more in their local project.

How to contact
Letter to above address. SAE required for written information

Address   The Green House
                    Hereford Street
                    Bedminster
                    Bristol BS3 4NA
Telephone   0117 923 1800
Fax   0117 923 1900

NATIONAL FEDERATION OF GATEWAY CLUBS

Provides activities and opportunities for people with learning disabilities

Gateway is a network of more than 700 clubs and projects for people with learning disabilities who live in England, Wales and Northern Ireland. Clubs and projects are run by volunteers (with staff support) who encourage users to reach their full potential. Gateway offers training and information to volunteers and users who want to learn new skills.

FREETIME

Address   Mencap National Centre
                   123 Golden Lane
                   London EC1Y 0RT
Telephone   0171 454 0454
Fax   0171 608 3254

NATIONAL FEDERATION OF YOUNG FARMERS CLUBS (NFYFC)

The services provided by YFCs include educational services eg courses, seminars, publications and training aids; many social functions; competitions held at regional and national level; the opportunity to travel via the international exchange programme; a wide range of sporting activities; encouragement for young people to take an interest in and express an opinion on farming and countryside issues.

Costs/waiting lists
Annual subscriptions vary between £5 and £10

Address   National Agricultural Centre
                   Stoneleigh Park
                   Kenilworth
                   Warwickshire CV8 2LG
Telephone   01203 696544
Fax   01203 696559
E-mail
gfc@nfyfc.org.uk

FREETIME

SCOUT ASSOCIATION, THE

Scouts are young men and women who take part in a very wide range of outdoor activities including climbing, abseiling, canoeing, sailing, hiking, mountaineering etc, as well as community work, international projects throughout the world, training in a variety of different areas and a personal development programme.

Age range
Venture Scouts 15-20 years, other sections 6-15 years
Costs/waiting lists
Subscriptions vary from group to group
Address   Baden-Powell House
               Queen's Gate
               London SW7 5JS
Telephone   0171 584 7030
Fax   0171 590 5103
E-mail
ukbphscout@aol.com
Web site
http://www.scoutbase.org.uk

SEA CADET CORPS (SCC)

The Sea Cadet Corps is a voluntary youth organisation comprised of 400 units scattered throughout the country, providing facilities for the Cadets to take part in activities in which self-discipline, leadership and a sense of responsibility to the community are encouraged. The accent is on the sea; sailing and boat work have a high priority and most units have access to water and boats. Other activities include band training, communications, engineering, model-making, swimming, visits to ships, expeditions and much more. All cadets can take part in adventure training, map-reading and the Duke of Edinburgh's Award Scheme.

Regional addresses
Six regional addresses – details available from Head Office
Numbers passing through
17,000 members
Costs/waiting lists
Voluntary monthly contribution. Part assistance with travel costs for selected field trips

Address	202 Lambeth Road
	London SE1 7JF
Telephone	0171 928 8978
Fax	0171 401 2537

FREETIME

SOCIETY FOR POPULAR ASTRONOMY
(SPA)

The SPA is open to beginners and more experienced amateur astronomers of all ages. There are four meetings each year in London and occasional meetings and weekend courses away from London. Publications include the *Popular Astronomy* magazine four times a year as well as news circulars, usually about six times a year. The society also provides a GCSE advisory service and an instrument advisory service, and society officials are pleased to correspond with young people to provide help and guidance. Members may contribute to specialist observing sections.

Age range
Any
Numbers passing through
Nearly 3,000 members
Costs/waiting lists
Annual UK subscription is £10 per year (under review – please enquire for current rate) which includes all publications. Weekend courses are charged at cost for accommodation, food etc
Address   36 Fairway
                Keyworth
                Nottingham NG12 5DU

FREETIME

ST JOHN AMBULANCE

Club with opportunities to learn everything from first aid to abseiling

As a member of St John Ambulance you can learn everything from first aid to abseiling, from camping to working in the community and much more. St John Cadets aim for a balance of fun and responsibility. You can participate in the Duke of Edinburgh's Award Scheme, gain valuable experience running your local St John Youth Council, and benefit from an exciting range of residential training programmes. There is also a St John society called Links, which operates in universities and higher and further education colleges.

How to contact
By letter or telephone to the Youth Services Department at National HQ or contact County HQ

Costs/waiting lists
Small weekly divisional subscription plus some uniform costs

Address	National Headquarters
	1 Grosvenor Crescent
	London SW1X 7EF
Telephone	0171 235 5231
Fax	0171 235 0796

FREETIME

WOODCRAFT FOLK

Woodcraft Folk activities are based around weekly group meetings for both boys and girls. Groups are divided into four age ranges: Elfins 6-9-year-olds, Pioneers 10-12-year-olds, Venturers 13-25-year-olds and District Fellowship 16-20-year-olds. Programmes may include games, drama, singing, dancing, craftwork, discussion and projects. Groups regularly hike, camp and enjoy other residential experiences. International understanding is an important part of the curriculum, which is supported by a large exchange programme.

Costs/waiting lists
Weekly subscription up to 16 is 40-50p. 16-17 annual subscription is £5 unwaged. 16+ unwaged is £8, waged £15

Address 13 Ritherdon Road
London SW17 8QE
Telephone 0181 767 9799
Fax 0181 767 2457
E-mail
folk_hou@woodcrft.demon.co.uk
Web site
http://www.poptel.org.uk/woodcraft

WRITE AWAY

Penfriend club for special needs children and young people in the UK

Pen friend club for special needs children and young people in the UK, and their brothers and sisters. Members can correspond using print, tapes, fax or E-mail. Parties and events are organised whereby the pen friends can meet. A magazine is produced each term.

Costs
£2.00 registration fee for three pen friends

Address	29 Crawford Street
	London W1H 1PL
Telephone	0171 724 0878
Fax	0171 723 1761
Minicom	0171 724 0878
E-mail	

writeaway@ndirect.co.uk

YOUNG ARCHAEOLOGISTS CLUB (YAC)

The YAC is the only national club of its kind for anyone between the ages of 9 and 16. Membership includes a pin badge and membership card which will entitle you to free discounted entry to centres around the country. You will also receive the club's exciting quarterly magazine *Young*

FREETIME

Archaeologist. YAC members can join local branches who organise regular activity-based events. Contact the Club Coordinator, Juliet Mather, at the address below for further details.

Numbers passing through
1,500 members
Costs/waiting lists
Membership is £7.50 per year
Address	Bowes Morrell House
	111 Walmgate
	York YO1 2UA
Telephone	01904 671417

E-mail
archaeology@compuserve.com
Web site
http://britac3.britac.ac.uk/cba

YOUTH CLUBS UK

Youth Clubs UK supports a national network of youth clubs throughout the UK, through 41 local associations and three divisions in Scotland, Northern Ireland and Wales. Youth Clubs UK organises a wide range of informal education, leisure activities and innovative community projects. Young people in the clubs have the opportunity to join the National Members Group, which represents young people's views in the management of Youth Clubs UK and gives opportunities for involvement in many community projects, representation of Youth Clubs UK abroad etc. Residential centre in the New Forest offers vacation courses with leisure activities and sports options.

Numbers passing through
600,000 in membership of clubs

Address	11 St Bride Street
	London EC4A 4AS
Telephone	0171 353 2366
Fax	0171 353 2369

Web site
http://web.ukonline.co.uk/youthclubs.uk/

FREETIME

ORGANISATIONS

BLACK ENVIRONMENT NETWORK (BEN)

Young people who belong to an ethnic minority group and want to do an environmental project can receive advice and information on the environment and apply for grants to carry out projects, for example, the Ethnic Minorities Award Scheme (EMAS). The leader of the project should, wherever possible, be from an ethnic minority as should some of the participants of the scheme.

Costs/waiting lists
The service is free and applications for funding should ideally be made 3-6 months in advance

Address	UK Office
	9 Llainwen Uchaf
	Llanberis, Gwynedd
	Wales LL55 4LL
Telephone	01286 870 715
Fax	01286 870 715

BRITISH TRUST FOR CONSERVATION VOLUNTEERS (BTCV)

BTCV is the UK's largest practical conservation charity, creating opportunities for over 84,000 volunteers each year to take practical action to protect their local environment. BTCV runs over 600 natural breaks and international conservation working holidays throughout the year. These offer the chance to meet people, learn new skills and most importantly have a great time. Examples of holidays include a bat bonanza in the Pennines, to enhance roosting sites and learn about bat ecology; managing the heathland habitats of the lizards and sand-burrowing wasps of the Wirral nature reserves; creating footpaths in a seashore national park on Cape Cod and a tree-planting safari in the mountainous deserts of Andalucia.

Regional addresses
BTCV has a network of over 90 field offices throughout England, Wales and Northern Ireland. Each office organises a wide range of weekday, weekend and week-long environmental projects

Age range
16+ for natural breaks. No age limit for local projects

Numbers passing through
84,000 volunteers each year. 6,000 people take part in natural breaks and international conservation working holidays

How to contact
For a free Natural Break or international conservation working holidays brochure phone 01491 824602

FREETIME

Costs/waiting lists

BTCV membership costs £12, concessions £6. Natural breaks start from £28 a week inclusive of food and accommodation. International conservation working holidays start at around £50 excluding travel. Early booking is recommended

Address	36 St Mary's Street
	Wallingford
	Oxfordshire OX10 0EU
Telephone	01491 839766
Fax	01491 839646

CATHEDRAL CAMPS

Volunteers do routine maintenance and simple conservation work on cathedrals and Christian buildings of architectural significance, carrying out both routine and sometimes more spectacular tasks under the guidance of craftsmen. Camps take place at different cathedrals between mid-July and early September and last for one week with volunteers working approximately 36 hours a week, 8.30am to 5pm each day. Food and accommodation are provided and volunteers sleep in the Cathedral hall or similar building. Each camp is run by a leader and two assistant leaders, and volunteers are asked to contribute to the social life of the camp and help with domestic duties on a rota basis.

FREETIME

Projects qualify under the Duke of Edinburgh's Award Scheme.

Numbers passing through
700
How to contact
By letter to Booking Secretary, Shelley Beny, at address below for brochures and bookings
Costs/waiting lists
The camp fee is £38. Local Education Authorities occasionally give grants but this is rare. Some bursaries are available from Cathedral Camps in cases of hardship/unemployment. Camps are usually over-subscribed and you are advised to apply early. Brochures for each year are available in February

Address	16 Glebe Avenue Flitwick Bedfordshire MK45 1HS
Telephone	01525 716237

CONSERVATION VOLUNTEERS – NORTHERN IRELAND (CVNI)

Organises conservation projects for volunteers in Northern Ireland

CVNI organises practical conservation projects for volunteers including residential week-long holidays (book via form in their brochure *The Natural Break*), residential weekends and training courses (book via form in their brochure *Conservation Opportunities*), access to NVQ 'Landscapes and Ecosystems', daily volunteering opportunities and the opportunity to become a 'Natural Pioneer' – an award of up to £3,000 to undertake a project helping the environment (minimum age 16, applicants must be UK citizens).

Address   Beech House
159 Ravenhill Road
Belfast
Northern Ireland BT6 0BP
Telephone 01232 645169
Fax 01232 6444 409
E-mail
cvni@btcv.org.uk
Web site
http://www.btcv.org.uk

CORAL CAY CONSERVATION EXPEDITIONS

Recruits volunteers to assist with coral reef and tropical forest conservation

The Coral Cay Conservation (CCC) recruits thousands of young people from all over the world to help survey and protect threatened coral reefs and rainforests in the Caribbean and Asia-Pacific. Volunteers are taught to scuba dive as well as a range of supportive skills, including coastal zone management, marine/forest ecology and species identification, survey techniques etc. Volunteers live and work as self-sufficient teams, often on remote coral islands for periods of 2-12 weeks. Expeditions depart for Indonesia, the Philippines and Belize throughout the year.

Costs

Volunteers must contribute to the costs of their expeditions. This ranges from £650 to £2850

Address	154 Clapham Park Road
	London SW4 7DE
Telephone	0171 498 6248
Fax	0171 498 8447

E-mail
ccc@coralcay.demon.co.uk
Web site
http://www.coralcay.org

EARTHWATCH EUROPE

Matches 'paying volunteers' with environmental research projects around the world

Earthwatch needs 'paying volunteers' to work with some of the world's leading scientists, to study some of the most pressing issues of our

FREETIME

time and to help achieve some amazing results. No special skills are required – just curiosity and willingness to give anything a go.

Costs/waiting lists

Membership is £25, paying for the catalogues and magazines you will receive. Most projects require participants to raise some funds for themselves – from £400 to £2,000. This becomes a donation that helps fund the project you join. Earthwatch can give some advice on sponsorship and fundraising

Address	57 Woodstock Road
	Oxford
	Oxon OX2 6HJ
Telephone	01865 311600
Fax	01865 311383

E-mail
info@uk.earthwatch.org
Web site
http://www.earthwatch.org

FRIENDS OF THE EARTH (FOE)

Provides opportunities to get involved with protecting the environment

Friends of the Earth involves young people in protecting the environment and in working for real change. It is one of the UK's leading environmental pressure groups, campaigning on a wide range of issues including pollution, transport, energy, waste, habitats, forests and sustainable development. They publish a range of up-to-date information on environmental issues including leaflets and books with plenty of ideas for what people can do to make a difference. They have over 250 local campaigning groups and campaign locally, nationally and internationally. For information on how to join, or your nearest local group or a free copy of their publications catalogue please write to the address below.

Address   26-28 Underwood Street
                London N1 7JQ
Telephone   0171 490 1555
Fax   0171 490 0881
E-mail
info@foe.co.uk
Web site
http://www.foe.co.uk

FREETIME

FRONTIER – THE SOCIETY FOR ENVIRONMENTAL EXPLORATION

Carries out conservation research in Uganda, Tanzania, Mozambique and Vietnam

Working with the host government, Frontier surveys remote and previously unexplored areas to help set up some form of environmental protection. Volunteers come out in ten-week expeditions to carry out the work either to gain experience for a career in conservation or simply to do something practical to help the environment whilst experiencing a totally different culture.

Costs/waiting lists

Participation in a ten-week expedition to East Africa or Vietnam would cost candidates approximately £2,900 which covers all expenses such as airfare, camp equipment, insurance, food, etc. This also includes a special briefing weekend held in England prior to departure. Advice will be given concerning the raising of funds. Candidates are advised to apply at least 4-6 months in advance

Address   77 Leonard Street
                 London EC2A 4QS
Telephone   0171 613 2422
Fax   0171 613 2992
E-mail
enquiries@frontier.mailbox.co.uk
Web site
http://www.mailbox.co.uk/frontier

HENRY FORD EUROPEAN CONSERVATION AWARDS FOR THE UK

Provide grants for conservation initiatives in Europe

The Ford European Conservation Awards, now in their 14th year in Europe, are for conservation initiatives undertaken by individuals or community groups in all European countries. Projects that involve young people, natural environment, national heritage and conservation engineering are all eligible. Entries will be judged by the Conservation Foundation panel, which will select the best projects. There will be a cash prize for the winners in each category.

How to contact
Send SAE for further information
Costs/waiting lists
The closing date is in the spring of each year.

Address	The Conservation Foundation
	1 Kensington Gore
	London SW7 2AR
Telephone	0171 591 3111

E-mail
conservef@gn.apc.org

FREETIME

LAND USE VOLUNTEERS (LUV)

Volunteer placements for those interested in gardening

If you have experience and/or basic qualifications in horticulture, have worked in some capacity ·with people with special needs, and are looking for a way to use your skills, LUV will help. They help projects use horticulture as therapy for people with disabilities by providing a volunteer with horticultural skills. You may help in preparing a new site for a horticultural therapy unit, or train clients and care staff in basic horticultural tasks. LUV will place you in a project that reflects your own particular skills and interests.

Address	c/o Horticultural Therapy
	Goulds Ground
	Vallis Way
	Frome
	Somerset BA11 3DW
Telephone	01373 464782
Fax	01373 464782

FREETIME

MARINE CONSERVATION SOCIETY

Provides volunteering opportunities and career information on marine conservation

Information on all aspects of marine conservation; factsheets for students and pupils including careers in marine sciences; surveys including beach-cleans and wildlife projects which encourage young people to take an active role, eg, Beachwatch, Ocean Vigil, Oceanwatch. Mail order sales of marine publications and gifts. Send SAE with all requests for information.

Regional addresses
List of local groups available from main office
Costs/waiting lists
Annual membership fee £15, Student/child £8
Address   9 Gloucester Road
                     Ross-on-Wye
                     Herefordshire HR9 5BU
Telephone   01989 566017
Fax   01989 567815
E-mail
mcsuk@mcmail.com
Web site
http://www.mcsuk.mcmail.com

FREETIME

MERLIN TRUST, THE

Gives grants to people with real love for plants and gardening

The Merlin Trust awards grants to people with a genuine interest in plants, gardens or gardening. Grants to date have been awarded to varying requests. Examples include:

A tour of botanic gardens in Ireland
A study of flower photography
A trip to Japan to study salad crops
The attendance of a conference about trees in Versailles

To read about the Merlin's achievements to date you are invited to read the personal reports which are in the Royal Horticulture Society's Lindley Library in London. (By appointment only 0171 821 3050) Applications for funding, which are welcome throughout the year, should be forwarded to Valerie Finnis, enclosing a large SAE.

Address   Valerie Finnis
                     The Merlin Trust
                     The Dower House
                     Boughton House
                     Kettering
                     Northamptonshire NN14 1BJ

Telephone   01536 482297
Fax   01536 482294

PEAK PARK CONSERVATION VOLUNTEERS (PPCV)

The National Park Ranger Service enables volunteers of all ages and backgrounds to become actively involved in many types of practical conservation projects throughout the Peak District National Park. The projects include footpath construction and erosion control, fencing, walling, tree-planting, scrub clearance, simple nature reserve management and much more. The project tasks are led by a Ranger/Supervisor and tools, materials and a lunchtime brew are provided. Tasks are arranged all year round for each weekend although limited opportunities exist during the midweek period.

Numbers passing through
Over 3,000 per year
Address   The Volunteers Organiser
                 Peak Park Joint
                 Planning Board
                 Aldern House
                 Baslow Road
                 Bakewell DE45 1AE
Telephone   01629 815 185
Fax   01629 815045

FREETIME

SCOTTISH CONSERVATION PROJECTS TRUST (SCP)

Involves people in improving the quality of the environment

Action Breaks are 7-14 day practical, residential conservation projects for people aged over 16 held throughout Scotland. Great fun, a good way to make new friends and learn new skills. There is a midweek group in Edinburgh which organises non-residential projects for mainly unemployed volunteers aged over 16. Volunteers need no experience. There are weekend training courses in environmental skills. There are also long term volunteering and leadership opportunities. SCP also runs a variety of other events throughout Scotland to involve young people in conservation work.

Costs/waiting lists

Student membership is £8. Action breaks cost £4 per day. There are no costs for midweek projects. Training courses cost £24 per weekend

Address	Balallan House
	24 Allan Park
	Stirling FK8 2QG
Telephone	01786 479697
Fax	01786 465359

WATERWAY RECOVERY GROUP (WRG)

Provides volunteers for restoration and conservation work on Britain's canals

WRG is the national organisation which arranges restoration and conservation work on Britain's canals and waterways. Work can vary from simple digging and clearing of old canal lines to complex reconstruction of original structures. There is work suitable for people of all ages and abilities and any training required will be given. You will find yourself working as part of a team of enthusiastic individuals and hopefully see a worthwhile result at the end of the day, as well as gaining skills and enjoying an entertaining social life. WRG is comprised of regional groups who work mainly at weekends on sites throughout the country. Groups currently active are WRG North West, WRG North East, WRG London and two 'non-aligned' groups who cover the rest of the country – WRG BITM (Bit in the Middle) and WRG NA (Navvies Anonymous). WRG also runs week-long canal camps to provide a major push to a particular canal restoration scheme. These are probably the best introduction to canal restoration and a booklet is available giving full details of these unique working holidays.

FREETIME

Costs/waiting lists
Annual subscription to magazine *Navvies* is a minimum of £1.50. Working weekends/weeks cost about £5 per day, which covers food and accommodation

Address   114 Regent's Park Road
                   London NW1 8UQ
Telephone   0171 722 7217
Fax   0171 722 7213
E-mail
wrg@waterway.demon.co.uk

WOMEN'S ENVIRONMENTAL NETWORK (WEN)

Educates, informs and empowers women who care about the environment

WEN researches and produces a range of action packs and briefings on all aspects of environmental issues. It relies on memberships and donations for its survival. Membership entitles you to receive newsletters, briefings and notice of public events, plus information on playing an active role. WEN encourages both men and women to join, but looks at environmental issues from a woman's perspective.

Costs
Membership ranges between £8 and £30

How to contact
Send a SAE with a 39p stamp for further information

Address	87 Worship Street
	London EC2A 2BE
Telephone	0171 247 3327
Fax	0171 247 4740

WWOOF

International exchange network to work on organic farms and small holdings

WWOOF is an exchange; in return for work on organic farms, gardens and small holdings, you receive meals, accommodation, the opportunity to learn and if necessary transport to the local station. WWOOF aims to provide first-hand experience of organic farming and growing, to get into the countryside, to help the organic movement which is labour intensive and does not rely on artificial fertilisers for fertility or persistent poisons for pest control, and to make contact with other people in the organic movement. Details of places throughout the UK needing help each weekend are listed in the newsletter which is sent to members every two months. Members can then make bookings for weekends or days of their choice and, if a place is available, will receive full details including travel information. The newsletter also gives details

FREETIME

of longer stays, events, developments training and job opportunities in the organic movement and includes members' contributions and advertisements. A detailed fix-it-yourself list of WWOOF places in the UK and overseas is also available to members who have satisfactorily completed at least two scheduled weekends, so that they can make their own arrangements to work, possibly for longer periods. Special arrangements can usually be made for those unable to complete two scheduled weekends.

How to contact
SAE to main office for brochure and application form
Costs/waiting lists
Annual membership is £10

Address	19 Bradford Road
	Lewes
	Sussex BN7 1RB
Telephone	01273 476286

PUBLICATIONS

WORKING WITH THE ENVIRONMENT

This book tells you all you need to know about the complete spectrum of environmental opportunities, including wildlife conservation, sustainable development, scientific research and eco-tourism. Explains how to go about finding a paid or voluntary job, part time or full time, in the UK or abroad and includes information on training and a comprehensive listing of relevant university courses.

Address	Vacation Work Publications
	9 Park End Street
	Oxford OX1 1HU
Telephone	01865 241 978
Fax	01865 790 885
Price	£9.99
ISBN	1 85458 148 1

FREETIME

EXPEDITIONS

ORGANISATIONS

BRATHAY EXPLORATION GROUP

Organises expeditions both in the UK and abroad

The Brathay Exploration Group offers a range of expeditions, courses and experiences led by volunteer leaders to locations from New Zealand to Shetland. It provides opportunities to increase environmental and cultural experiences and understanding through adventure, exploration and personal development projects in the UK and throughout the world. Annually, some 12 expeditions are available to young people. Within the programme, objectives, duration, locations and fees vary enabling a wide range of people to participate.

Costs/waiting lists
The Trust, through the organisation, offers limited bursary funding to help reduce fees

Address   Brathay Hall
                  Ambleside
                  Cumbria LA22 0HP
Telephone   015394 33942
Fax   015394 33942

BSES EXPEDITIONS

Provide opportunities to join exploratory projects in remote areas of the world

The expeditions aim to combine the excitement of living under testing conditions with the research and production of valuable scientific work. Adventure expeditions can include mountaineering, sea kayaking, trekking, skiing, diving and caving. Science expeditions include earth and life sciences. Previous expeditions have been to the Himalayas, Arctic Norway, Namibia and Greenland. Applicants need to be physically fit and interested in science. Applicants should have plenty of enthusiasm, determination, common sense, the ability to work as a member of a team and a good sense of humour.

How to contact
By letter with SAE (A4 – with 31p stamp) for information, leaflets and application form
Costs/waiting lists
Each applicant will need to fundraise between £2,000 and £3,000, depending on which expedition they join

FREETIME

Address	c/o Royal Geographical
	Society
	1 Kensington Gore
	London SW7 2AR
Telephone	0171 591 3141
Fax	0171 591 3140

EXPEDITION ADVISORY CENTRE

The Expedition Advisory Centre can provide information, advice, training and publications for anyone planning or wishing to join a scientific or adventurous expedition overseas. This includes an annual seminar in November on 'Planning a Small Expedition' plus other meetings on expedition fundraising, leadership, medicine and field research techniques. The EAC at the Royal Geographical Society publishes various books of interest to young people thinking of becoming involved in an expedition or travel, either through a structured organisation such as Operation Raleigh, or independently.

Joining an Expedition – how to take advantage of the expedition opportunities offered by over 50 UK-based organisations, with fundraising advice (price £5.00)

Fundraising to Join an Expedition – a guide for those raising funds required to join ventures such as Operation Raleigh (price £2.50)

FREETIME

Sources of Information for Independent Travellers – where to get the best information on health, equipment, visas, insurance, maps etc (price £5.00)

Expedition Planners Handbook and Directory – for those organising adventurous and scientific projects overseas (price £12.95)

Age range
Any
Numbers passing through
10,000+ enquiries per year
Costs/waiting lists
Details of costs of publications, courses and seminars available from address below. Replies usually within 21 days

Address	Royal Geographical Society
	1 Kensington Gore
	London SW7 2AR
Telephone	0171 591 3030
Fax	0171 591 3031

E-mail
eac@rgs.org
Web site
http://www.rgs.org/eac

FREETIME

RALEIGH INTERNATIONAL

Raleigh International is a charity which aims to develop young people by giving them the opportunity to carry out demanding environmental and community projects in the UK and remote parts of the world. Raleigh is recruiting over 1,000 young people between the ages of 17 and 25 and over 350 members of staff aged over 25 for expeditions in 1996/97 to Chile, Zimbabwe, Uganda, Belize and Malaysia. No skills are necessary except the ability to swim and speak basic English. Raleigh have expedition schemes for young people at risk, for international applicants and for 'commercial venturers' who are sponsored by their companies, as well as for standard applicants from the UK.

How to contact
Send an A4 SAE to Head Office
Costs/waiting lists
Participants are asked to raise between £500 and £2,950 through sponsorship and fundraising events. Many companies send employees as part of a training programme and there are a number of grants available from Training Enterprise Councils, Local Authorities and charitable trusts

Address	Raleigh House
	27 Parsons Green Lane
	London SW6 4HZ
Telephone	0171 371 8585
Fax	0171 371 5116

E-mail
info@raleigh.org.uk

WINSTON CHURCHILL MEMORIAL TRUST

Funds air fares and expenses for overseas travel, if benefiting you and your country

Travelling fellowships awarded to UK citizens to travel overseas with air fares and expenses paid for projects which will benefit you and your country on your return (awards do not cover courses or academic studies).

Numbers passing through
100 fellowships are given each year
How to contact
Telephone or letter (with SAE) for information on how to apply
Costs/waiting lists
Apply from July to October to travel the following year

Address	15 Queen's Gate Terrace
	London SW7 5PR
Telephone	0171 584 9315
Fax	0171 581 0410

FREETIME

WORLD CHALLENGE EXPEDITIONS

Organises expeditions involving project work and gap-year work placements

World Challenge Expeditions is a specialist in developmental youth adventure. As well as its school schemes, it provides opportunities for individuals. Gap Challenge for individuals, formerly Fill the Gap, provides 3-6 month voluntary and paid work placements for gap-year students. Voluntary work placements are available in India, Nepal, Tanzania, Zanzibar, Malawi, Ecuador, Belize and South Africa. In India and Nepal, Gap Challenge students teach at secondary schools and homes for the disabled in the Kulu Valley in Goa, Kathmandu and Pokhara. In Nepal, there is also the opportunity for students to be seconded to trekking agencies for the Learning for Leadership Programmes. In Tanzania, Malawi, Belize and Zanzibar, Gap Challenge students teach basic English, science and geography to secondary school students. In South Africa they work for the Leonard Cheshire Foundation in their homes for the disabled and in Ecuador students work on conservation projects in the northern rain forests. Paid work is available in Canada and Australia. In Canada, students can earn money at hotels and mountain lodges in Banff and Jasper in the Rockies. In Australia students can earn basic pocket money working on cattle sheep and trail ride farms.

Costs
These vary according to expedition
Costs/waiting lists
Work placements cost approximately £1,500 (including a selection course, specialist training course and 12-month open return air fare). This price varies according to programme and destination

Address	Black Arrow House
	2 Chandos Road
	London NW10 6NF
Telephone	0181 961 1122
Fax	0181 961 1551
E-mail	

welcome@world-challenge.co.uk

YOUNG EXPLORERS' TRUST (YET)

Advises people wanting to go on and organise an expedition

YET is an advisory body concerned with youth expeditions. It provides advice and contacts for groups and individuals planning expeditions, mainly abroad. Whilst YET does not plan expeditions itself, it can put individuals in touch with those who do. YET also runs an approval and grant aid scheme (Jim Bishop Memorial Trust) for youth

FREETIME

expeditions (groups not individuals) to remote areas overseas.

Regional addresses
Extensive network of local contacts, but initial contact should be made through main office
Costs/waiting lists
There are no costs for using YET service

Address	Stretton Cottage
	Wellow Road
	Ollerton
	Newark, Notts NG22 9AX
Telephone	01623 861027
Fax	01623 861027

PUBLICATIONS

TRAVELLERS' SURVIVAL KIT SERIES

This series of guides cover India, South Africa, Lebanon, Australia, New Zealand, Russia and the Republics, Western Europe, Eastern Europe, the East (Turkey to Indonesia), Cuba, South America, Central America, USA and Canada. They give you the low-down on what to do and see, money, travel and where to stay. Prices range from around £7 to £10.

Address	Vacation Work Publications
	9 Park End Street
	Oxford OX1 1HU
Telephone	01865 241 978
Fax	01865 790 885

YEAR BETWEEN, A

A guide for those taking a gap year between school and higher education

A Year Between provides full details of over 100 organisations offering placements in industry, research, business, teaching, community, social service and youth work in Britain and overseas. Authoritative advice and information is included together with practical hints, discussion of the pros and cons, and details on planning and preparation.

FREETIME

Address	Central Bureau for Educational Visits & Exchanges 10 Spring Gardens London SW1A 2BN
Telephone	0171 389 4004
Fax	0171 389 4426
Price	£8.99
ISBN	0 90008 798 6

FREETIME

COMMUNITY SERVICE VOLUNTEERS (CSV)

Community Service Volunteers invites all young people to experience the challenge, excitement and reward of helping people in need. Every year 3,000 volunteers work throughout the UK with elderly people, adults with disabilities, children who are disabled, in care or in trouble, and homeless people. Volunteers work hard, have fun, and gain valuable experience. Volunteers work away from home, full time, from 4-12 months and receive full board, lodging, and a weekly allowance. Applications are welcome throughout the year, and no previous experience or qualifications are needed. No volunteer is ever rejected.

Costs/waiting lists

No costs involved for information or to take up placements. Usually takes 6-8 weeks to place volunteers after application

Address	237 Pentonville Road
	London N1 9NJ
Telephone	0171 278 6601
Fax	0171 837 9621

FREETIME

CONCORDIA (YSV) LTD

Concordia offers volunteering opportunities in Europe.

How to contact
SAE for leaflets and information
Costs/waiting lists
Enrolment fees are £70. Volunteers are expected to pay their own travel costs. Contact in spring when project details become available. Concordia also requires UK-based people over the age of 20 to lead projects in the UK

Address	Heversham House
	20-22 Boundary Road
	Hove BN3 4ET
Telephone	01273 422218
Fax	01273 422218

INTERNATIONAL VOLUNTARY SERVICE (IVS)

Organises international work camps for 2-3 weeks

IVS aims to promote, peace, justice and international understanding through voluntary work. IVS is the British branch of Service Civil International (SCI), a worldwide organisation with branches in over 30 countries. Our main activity is the organisation of work camps, bringing people together to support local community projects. These are often practical projects – renovation, restoration, conservation, environmental work or work with children or people with disabilities. Living and working together in such groups can help to break down gaps between peoples and cultures. Most of the projects take place in Great Britain, Eastern and Western Europe, North Africa and North America.

Address	Old Hall
	East Bergholt
	Colchester CO7 6TQ
Telephone	01206 298215
Fax	01206 299043

FREETIME

NATIONAL ASSOCIATION OF VOLUNTEER BUREAUX – NAVB

Volunteer Bureaux are local voluntary organisations specialising in giving advice and information on all aspects of volunteering. They enable people to get involved in a wide range of 'voluntary action'. Volunteer Bureaux interview and advise would-be volunteers about the whole range of volunteering activities in their communities.

Address	New Oxford House
	Waterloo Street
	Birmingham B2 5UG
Telephone	0121 633 4555
Fax	0121 633 4043

NATIONAL CENTRE FOR VOLUNTEERING

Signposts database listing volunteering opportunities by postcode

The Volunteer Centre can provide a print-out on volunteering opportunities in different areas across the country. The service is free. Volunteers aged over 18 can get information sheets about volunteering overseas and residential volunteering in the UK.

How to contact
By letter (with SAE) to the Advice and

Information department for further information on volunteering

Address   Carriage Row
                 183 Eversholt Street
                 London NW1 1BU
Telephone   0171 388 9888
Fax   0171 383 0448
E-mail
voluk@aol.com

PRINCE'S TRUST VOLUNTEERS, THE

Volunteering opportunities

A national programme which provides young people with the opportunity for personal development training and experience while working with and in their local community. Each 15-strong team of volunteers includes a full mix of young people from different backgrounds, all walks of life and those who are employed, unemployed or in education. Each team participates in a programme which includes team building, residential experience and individual placements and team project work in the community. These community opportunities will include environmental and caring experiences. Participation is usually 60 days, but can be shorter time periods. Volunteers who successfully complete the programme receive a City and Guilds Profile of Achievement, a Prince's Trust Volunteers Certificate and the opportunity during the programme to attain personal skills qualifications such as the Community Sports Leader Award and a First Aid Certificate.

Numbers passing through
4,000 per year

Address	18 Park Street East
	London NW1 4LH
Telephone	0800 842842 (freephone)

TOC H

Toc H offers community-based projects and events

Toc H runs short term residential projects throughout the year in the UK and Belgium, usually from a weekend up to three weeks in duration. Project work undertaken can include work with people with various disabilities; work with children in need; play schemes and camps; conservation and manual work; study and/or discussion sessions. The projects offer participants opportunities to learn more about themselves and the world we live in.

Costs/waiting lists
Registration fees range from £5-£15

FREETIME

according to the length of stay and some events require a small additional fee. Toc H raises money to enable volunteers to pay as little as possible. Places are offered on a first-come-first-served basis

Address   1 Forest Close
                     Wendover
                     Aylesbury
                     Buckinghamshire HP22 6BT
Telephone   01296 623911
Fax   01296 696137

VENTURE SCOTLAND

Runs outdoor-based activity courses

Venture Scotland is a voluntary organisation which utilises the skills of volunteers to run outdoor-based personal development programmes. Their client group, 'participants', are from backgrounds in which their access to such opportunities is limited. The core service provided is the 'Bothy Venture' programme of two volunteer-led weekends. A remote bothy (mountain hut) in Glen Etive is the base from which a combination of outdoor and environmental activities takes place. Every programme is delivered by 5-6 volunteers. In addition to the 'Bothy Venture' programme, they pursue longer term developmental aims for volunteers and young adults by accessing a

FREETIME

range of 'follow-on' and training opportunities. These can be in-house ie volunteer led, or through their established network of complementary agencies.

Costs/waiting lists
Weekend residential course fee is £20. This fee is negotiable if participants cannot afford it

Address   Bonnington Mill
                    72 Newhaven Road
                    Edinburgh EH6 5QG
Telephone   0131 553 5333
Fax   0131 553 5333

VOLUNTARY SERVICE BELFAST (VSB)

Recruits, places, supports and trains volunteers

Voluntary Service Belfast's Volunteer Centre provides a link between people who wish to become involved in voluntary work and organisations and individuals who can benefit from the services provided by volunteers. Volunteering opportunities exist with older people and the disabled, children and those most in need. Also opportunities available for practical tasks such as painting, decorating and conservation work. Volunteers can gain practical experience, comprehensive training leading to nationally-recognised

FREETIME

qualifications and opportunities to learn new skills.

Address	70-72 Lisburn Road
	Belfast
	Northern Ireland BT9 6AF
Telephone	01232 200850
Fax	01232 200860

VOLUNTEER DEVELOPMENT SCOTLAND (VDS)

VDS is the national resource and development agency on volunteering in Scotland. It mainly provides support services to agencies and individuals who work with volunteers. It also holds information about volunteer bureaux in Scotland so although it is unable to advise on individual placements it can point potential volunteers in the right direction.

Costs/waiting lists

There are no costs for information

Address	72 Murray Place
	Stirling FK8 2BX
Telephone	01786 479593
Fax	01786 447148
E-mail	

vds@vds.org.uk

FREETIME

WESTON SPIRIT, THE

The Weston Spirit experience lasts for approximately one year and is something that can be done alongside whatever else you are doing. It is completely voluntary and you need no special skills or abilities – only a willingness to take part. There are lots of opportunities offered on many different levels; personal, social and educational amongst others. Members have the chance to make many new friends as well as learning lots of new things in a relaxed, informal, fun and supportive environment.

Regional addresses
Merseyside, 85a Bold Street, Liverpool L1 4HF Tel: 0151 707 0821
South Glamorgan, 1 Guildford Crescent, Cardiff CF1 4HJ Tel: 01222 232992
Tyneside, 5 Charlotte Square, Newcastle-upon-Tyne NE1 4XF Tel: 0191 232 1322
Age range
16-18 at recruitment
Numbers passing through
180 per year

Address	2 Roscoe Place
	Bold Street
	Liverpool L1 4HF
Telephone	0151 709 6620
Fax	0151 707 0577

FREETIME

PUBLICATIONS

VOLUNTEER WORK

Guide to voluntary service

This guide advises on projects worldwide, detailing countries of operation, qualifications and skills required, terms and conditions of work. Includes insights from returned volunteers and advice on preparation, development issues, travel and health.

For further information

	Central Bureau for Educational Visits & Exchanges
	10 Spring Gardens
	London SW1A 2BN
Telephone	0171 389 4004
Fax	0171 389 4426
Price	£8.99
ISBN	1 89860 104 6

FREETIME

WEB SITES

VOLUNTEERING AND CHARITY ORGANISATIONS LISTING

A huge listing of volunteering and charity organisations

Web site
http://www.open.gov.uk/index/ficharty.htm

WORKING ABROAD & HOLIDAY WORK

ORGANISATIONS

ACTION ABROAD

Provides organised voluntary teaching placements in the developing world

Action Abroad sends out volunteers to organised 3-6 month placements to countries including Nepal, Uganda and Peru. The placements have been carefully selected in order to present those selected with as challenging a set up as possible. Placements begin in February and June every year. Action Abroad is highly selective due to popularity. It requires responsible people to teach, inspire confidence and relate well within different cultures and communities.

Costs
£185 placement fee plus all travel insurance and visa. All board and lodgings are organised and provided for

Address	Barley Farm
	Wrington
	Avon BS18 7SR
Telephone	01934 862 047
Fax	01635 269 345

FREETIME

AFRICA VENTURE

Opportunity for school-leavers to teach for four months in Africa

The Africa Venture scheme combines constructive and rewarding work with travel opportunities. Volunteers are placed in pairs primarily as assistant teachers in selected schools in Kenya, Zimbabwe, Uganda and Malawi for one term. Africa Venture provides good management throughout with emphasis on individual selection, in-country briefing and in-country support from the regional directors. You are advised to apply as early as possible as lists can close the previous November to departure.

Costs
Approximately £1,975 not including air fares. Africa Venture gives advice on fundraising

Address	10 Market Place
	Devizes
	Wiltshire SN10 1HT
Telephone	01380 729 009
Fax	01380 720 060

E-mail
aventure@aol.com
Web site
http://members.aol.com/aventure

BRITISH UNIVERSITIES NORTH AMERICA CLUB (BUNAC)

Organises work and travel programmes overseas for students

BUNAC is a non-profit-making organisation which enables students and young people to travel and work in America, Canada and Australia through various programmes. The largest of these is 'BUNACAMP' Counsellors which places people aged between 19 and 35 as counsellors on American children's summer camps to teach a wide variety of activities from mid-June to mid/end August and allows time to travel for up to six weeks afterwards. There are also general work and travel programmes mainly for students and gap-year students in America, Canada and Australia.

Regional addresses
There are voluntary representatives at most university campuses

Age range
Programmes are mainly aimed at university and gap-year students. However, BUNACAMP Counsellors is open to anyone aged between 19 and 35

How to contact
Send your name and address on a postcard to the London address requesting a *Working*

FREETIME

Adventures Worldwide brochure or telephone with any enquiries

Costs/waiting lists

Costs of the schemes vary but all programmes are designed to be self-financing so participants can recover the costs of travelling abroad by working once they arrive

Address	16 Bowling Green Lane
	London EC1R 0BD
Telephone	0171 251 3472
Fax	0171 251 0215

E-mail

bunac@easynet.co.uk

Web site

http://www.bunac.org

CAMP AMERICA

Recruits staff to work on summer camps or with American families in the USA

Camp America is looking for young people to work as youth leaders at American children's summer camps. Preferably you will have skills to teach activities such as sports, arts and crafts, drama etc. You don't need to be an expert to apply. Camp America provides free London to New York return flight; pocket money; board and lodging at camp; J1 cultural exchange visa and time for independent travel after your nine-week placement. Camp maintenance positions and family companion placements also available.

Address	37a Queen's Gate
	London SW7 5HR
Telephone	0171 581 7373
Fax	0171 581 7377
E-mail	

brochure@campamerica.co.uk

CAREERS EUROPE

Careers Europe produces a series of over 250 leaflets covering all aspects of working, studying and training within the European Union

Careers Europe is a publisher of a wide range of materials helping you make the most of the opportunities now available in Europe. This includes the Euroguides series, whose titles include *Finding Work in France, Law Careers in the EU* and *Teaching English in Europe*. Careers Europe also produces a series of over 250 leaflets covering all aspects of working, studying and training within the European Union, Eurofacts are available individually or as a set. Other information available from Careers Europe includes the Careers Europe Database, a European and International Careers Database and a series of training materials for schools, college and careers services.

FREETIME

Costs/waiting lists
Depending on the product
Address   4th Floor
    Midland House
    14 Cheapside
    Bradford BD1 4JA
Telephone   01274 829600
Fax   01274 829610
Web site
http://www.careuro.demon.co.uk/

EURAUPAIR UK

Provides au pairs with jobs in the USA for one-year contracts

EurAuPair is a programme initiated by ASSE International in order to give young Europeans a chance to spend a year as an au pair in America within a reliable and secure organisation. Full references are required for baby-sitters. Otherwise you can expect to do 45 hours per week of childcare, living with the family. You get full support from EurAuPair and two weeks paid holiday (pay is $118.25US per week), plus one weekend off per month. Departures are monthly except in February and December. Other EurAuPair offices are in Austria, Denmark, Finland, France, Germany, Italy, Netherlands, Norway, Portugal, Spain and Sweden.

FREETIME

Costs
$500 deposit towards training and flight must
be given but this will be refunded as long as
the one-year contract is completed and on
return to the UK

Address   17 Wheatfield Drive
                   Shifnal
                   Shropshire TF11 8HL
Telephone   01952 460733
Fax   01952 416850

FEDERATION OF RECRUITMENT AND EMPLOYMENT SERVICES (FRES)

FRES is the association for private recruitment
industry in the UK. A number of FRES
agencies specialise in employment
opportunities in Europe and further afield.
Such opportunities are usually for highly-
skilled applicants only. FRES also has
specialist au pair agencies in membership,
who are able to help those wishing to live
abroad as part of a family.

How to contact
Write to the above address to request a copy
of the FRES Overseas List and enclose a £2
postal order plus SAE. There is no charge for
the au pair list but please send SAE

FREETIME

Address	36-38 Mortimer Street
	London W1N 7RB
Telephone	0171 323 4300

GAP ACTIVITY PROJECTS LTD (GAP)

GAP offers work opportunities overseas for young people aged between 18 and 19 in their gap year

GAP offers work opportunities overseas for young people aged between 18 and 19 in their gap year between school and higher education or training. Placements are usually for 6-9 months, thereby leaving time for travel. GAP operates in over 30 different countries and the type of work varies from teaching English as a foreign language through to conservation work and social/community work.

Numbers passing through
1,000 placements out of 2,000 applications
Costs/waiting lists
£20 registration fee on application to cover administrative costs. On selection volunteers pay a GAP fee which is currently £375, and additional costs for insurance and medical requirements. A one- or two-week TEFL course (approx £100-£150) is required for English teaching. Once at the placement, volunteers receive free board and lodging

and, in most cases, pocket money. Students need to apply as early as possible, during their last year at school, preferably in September or October. The closing date for applications is 1 February each year

Address	44 Queen's Road
	Reading
	Berkshire RG1 4BB
Telephone	01734 594914
Fax	01734 576634

HEALTH PROJECTS ABROAD (HPA)

Opportunities to participate in a development education programme in Tanzania

Volunteers spend three months in rural Tanzania working with local communities to provide vital facilities such as health clinics. Pre-departure training weekends offer the chance to learn about the culture and language of the country. No particular skills are needed, other than the ability to work in a team and to learn from new experiences. Training and support are provided to help volunteers reach their target.

How to contact
Send SAE to above address, telephone, fax or E-mail for further information

FREETIME

Costs/waiting lists

Each volunteer must raise £2,900 as a contribution to their air fares, food, accommodation and travel and to the cost of running the projects

Address	PO Box 24
	Bakewell
	Derbyshire DE45 1ZW
Telephone	01629 640053
Fax	01629 640054
E-mail	

HPAUK@dial.pipex.com

INDIAN VOLUNTEERS FOR COMMUNITY SERVICE (IVCS)

Places you in projects in India, to learn about rural life and development work

Applicants are placed initially in a selected rural development project in north India for two to three weeks as observers and paying guests. After this period of adjustment and orientation they are given a choice of other projects to move on to. Some of these projects will accept applicants in some sort of volunteering capacity for longer periods. Length of stay is flexible. No placements are possible between April and beginning of September.

Numbers passing through
60-70
How to contact
SAE, phone or E-mail
Costs/waiting lists
Annual membership fee of £15 to IVCS. If selected, a further payment, which includes two-three weeks' board and lodging at the initial project, an orientation day and printed material. Individuals are responsible for their own air fares, travel in India and pocket money. Past applicants have raised money through local appeals and sponsored events. Must apply three months in advance

Address	12 Eastleigh Avenue
	Harrow
	Middlesex HA2 0UF
Telephone	0181 864 4740
E-mail	

endah@dircon.co.uk

INTERNATIONAL ASSOCIATION FOR THE EXCHANGE OF STUDENTS FOR TECHNICAL EXPERIENCE (IAESTE)

Provides course-related paid work placements for degree-level students

IAESTE is an independent, non-political worldwide organisation which arranges course-related paid work placements for degree-level students in fields such as

FREETIME

engineering, sciences, agriculture and the applied arts. Most last for up to 12 weeks during the summer, although longer placements may be available. Contact the Central Bureau at the address below for more information.

Address	The Central Bureau for Education & Exchange 10 Spring Gardens London SW1A 2BN
Telephone	0171 389 4774/4114
Fax	0171 389 4426
Web site	

http://www.britcoun.org/cbeve

KIBBUTZ REPRESENTATIVES

Organises working holidays on Kibbutz in Israel

Kibbutz Representatives give you an opportunity to live and work on a Kibbutz in Israel. A Kibbutz is a cooperative community and in exchange for working you will be provided with accommodation, meals and all the leisure facilities and activities of the Kibbutz. Occasional trips around the country will be arranged and a small allowance provided to cover essentials. You need to be in good physical and mental health, have at least six weeks to spare and be interested in participating in an alternative and communal lifestyle.

How to contact
SAE to address below for information and application forms

Costs/waiting lists
Approximate cost is £335 which includes a return air fare, insurance, registration fee and transfer to the Kibbutz. You need to apply about two months before you wish to go

Address	1a Accommodation Road London NW11 8ED
Telephone	0181 458 9235
Fax	0181 455 7930
E-mail	

enquiries@kibbutz.org.uk

PROJECT 67

Organises Kibbutz and Moshav placements for prospective volunteers

Project '67 'takes the worry out of travelling' by offering young people a package that takes care of everything. On a Kibbutz volunteers work an eight-hour day, six-day week in return for free accommodation, meals, laundry, recreational and social facilities, occasional trips and pocket money. On a Moshav work is mostly agricultural and volunteers work a minimum eight-hour day,

FREETIME

231

six-day week for a monthly wage and free shared self-contained accommodation. Project '67 arranges the flights, insurance and placement for volunteers and it also has its own office in Tel Aviv which can take care of the needs of volunteers while they are in Israel. Departures are all year round and the minimum stay is eight weeks.

How to contact

For more details those interested can call in to Project's London office to watch a video and have a chat with one of the staff, otherwise telephone or send SAE for a brochure

Costs/waiting lists

The cost is from £271 for Moshav and £291 for Kibbutz. Prices include return flight, airport taxes, insurance, one night in Tel Aviv Youth Hostel bed and breakfast and work placement. Volunteers can also purchase a 12-month open return with their package for an extra £20. Usually no waiting lists except in summer holiday periods

Address	10 Hatton Garden
	London EC1N 8AH
Telephone	0171 831 7626
Fax	0171 404 5588
E-mail	

moshav@aol.com

PROJECT TRUST

Sends young volunteers overseas for 12 months

Project Trust is an educational trust that places volunteers overseas each year in posts where they have the opportunity to do useful work for a year between school and higher education. Since 1968 it has sent over 3,000 volunteers to 39 different countries. Project aims to give young people a better understanding of the world outside Europe through living and working overseas. The three main categories of project are teacher-aides, social services and outdoor activities. Projects are chosen which do not take work from a local person, and which offer work that is both satisfying to the volunteer and useful to the host nation.

Costs/waiting lists

The average cost is about £3,850. Project Trust provides about £500; volunteers need to raise £3,175. The Trust has a finance officer who can advise how to go about fundraising, through sponsored events, charities, industry, local business etc. Projects start in August/September and you can apply 18 months before. Applications usually close in the previous November

FREETIME

Address	The Hebridean Centre
	Isle of Coll
	Argyll
	Scotland PA78 6TE
Telephone	01879 230444
Fax	01879 230357
E-mail	

projecttrust@compuserve.com

SCHOOLS PARTNERSHIP WORLDWIDE

Overseas teaching placements and environmental programmes for young people

Schools Partnership Worldwide was set up to organise placements for young people wanting to work in developing countries. Its main purpose is to provide them with challenging experiences outside formal education and focus their efforts on developing countries where educational and social services are poor. This aim is activated through:

– teaching and social programmes where the young person works as a teaching assistant providing English language support, and organising extra curricular activities.

– environmental programmes, where a group of young people from the North is matched with a group of young people from the country being targeted and they spend time learning about and acting upon important environmental issues. These programmes generally involve working with a local non-governmental organisation. During the programmes volunteers are also involved in spending funds raised in the West, on mini-projects to benefit the schools and local communities where they are working. Examples of such projects include:

– levelling and equipping playing fields, setting up poultry, piggery and bee-keeping projects, and setting up libraries. These projects are intended to benefit and involve as many young people as possible.

Volunteering
SPW programmes are open to young people aged between 18 and 25. Usually participants are taking a year out before, during or after further education. Local African and Nepali volunteers are recruited on the same basis as their European counterparts. There is an optional school sponsorship scheme through which schools agree to provide financial support for their pupils who wish to go away with SPW.

Expenses
The cost of teaching programmes is about £1,000-£1,750. This includes expenses such as travel, insurance, inoculations, and £750

FREETIME

sponsorship which provides basic living allowance, training and administration overseas – any remaining money is put into a Project Fund. The environmental programmes cost about £2,250 – this includes all of the above and £500 sponsorship for a local volunteer. All volunteers are asked to raise extra money to contribute towards mini development projects which they carry out while abroad.

Applications procedure

Details about applying and about the school sponsorship scheme can be obtained from the Director. Pre-departure and in-country training sessions are obligatory. Basic language and TEFL training is given.

Address	17 Dean's Yard
	London SW1P 3PB
Telephone	0171 222 0138/ 976 8070
Fax	0171 233 0008/ 963 1006

SHORT TERM EXPERIENCE PROGRAMMES

Organises programmes for volunteers to work with the local church – UK and abroad

Volunteers work for 6-12 months in placements either in Britain or Africa/Asia/South America. We also welcome applicants both from overseas and in Britain.

The practical tasks that volunteers are involved in vary widely from placement to placement. Examples include youthwork, community work, teaching, administration, and, if appropriate, use of volunteers' specialised skills. Volunteers overseas are usually placed as individuals or occasionally in pairs. In Britain, volunteers are placed with three or four others in small teams or communities.

Costs

Volunteers overseas will need to raise their own funds for living costs

Address	USPG
	Partnership House
	157 Waterloo Road
	London SE1 8XA
Telephone	0171 928 8681
Fax	0171 928 2371

STAGIAIRES

European Civil Service

Helps people find careers with the European Civil Service, in any age group.

Address	UK Office of the European
	Commission
	Information Office
	Jean Monnet House

8 Storey's Gate
London SW1P 3AT
Telephone 0171 973 1992
Fax 0171 973 1900
Web site
http://www.cec.org.uk

UNITED NATIONS ASSOCIATION (WALES) INTERNATIONAL YOUTH SERVICE

UNA (Wales) IYS is concerned with promoting the ideals of the United Nations

UNA (Wales) IYS is concerned with promoting the ideals of the United Nations Charter through the medium of short term International Voluntary Projects. These are split into the standard exchange programme running in Europe, North America, North Africa, Japan and Australia, with projects lasting between two and three weeks with no skills required; the 'North-South' programme for volunteers wishing to attend a project in Sub-Saharan Africa, Latin America or India, with projects lasting from four weeks up to six months, attendance at an IYS Orientation Weekend being compulsory and, for some organisations, relevant skills being required; and the Wales programme, which requires volunteers to act as 'leaders' (coordinators) for the groups of international volunteers coming to Wales.

FREETIME

How to contact

Write to the address below with an SAE. The list of International Projects comes out in March/April annually, North-South orientation weekends in February and October. Leaders training begins in April

Costs/waiting lists

Standard exchange projects cost between £70-£90 each. This will include accommodation and food while on the project

Address	Welsh Centre for International Affairs The Temple of Peace Cathays Park Cardiff CF1 3AP
Telephone	01222 223088
Fax	01222 665557

WINANT CLAYTON VOLUNTEER ASSOCIATION (WCVA)

Working with deprived inner-city kids and AIDS patients in the USA

WCVA provides an opportunity for people of all ages and backgrounds to experience another culture and people, by working within it for a period of three months from June to September each summer. Placements vary and examples include working with deprived inner-city kids; working with AIDS

FREETIME

239

patients; helping in a children's home; working in an adult psychiatric rehabilitation centre. All placements are on the east coast of America. Some voluntary experience in the UK would be useful but maturity and keenness are more important.

Costs/waiting lists
Volunteers usually need £500 to pay for air fare and insurance and a further £500 to finance their three-week holiday at the end of their placement. Individuals often fundraise locally or apply to charities such as the Rotary Club, Round Table, Prince's Trust etc. Volunteers should apply from September to January before the summer they wish to travel

Address   The Davenant Centre
179 Whitechapel Road
London E1 1DU
Telephone   0171 375 0547
Fax   0171 377 2437

WINGED FELLOWSHIP TRUST

Organises respite holidays, trips overseas for people with severe disabilities

The Winged Fellowship Trust organises respite breaks and holidays in five purpose-built centres in the UK. They also arrange trips overseas for people with severe physical disabilities. Every year the Winged Fellowship

Trust needs approximately 6,000 volunteers, the majority of whom are young people – students or unemployed. The volunteers are required to become companions/carers for disabled people.

Address	Angel House
	20-32 Pentonville Road
	London N1 9XD
Telephone	0171 833 2594
Fax	0171 278 0370

E-mail
wft@ukonline.co.uk
Web site
http://web.ukonline.co.uk/members/wft

YEAR OUT EMPLOYMENT OPPORTUNITIES

Offers gap-year employment to students who wish to take a year out between A-levels and further education

Towers Perrin is an international firm of consulting actuaries and management consultants offering gap-year employment to students who wish to take a year out between A-levels and university. Employment is from 1 September until mid-May of the following year. Gap-year students will work in either the Property Casualty or Employee Benefit Services unit. The work will appeal to students

FREETIME

with a strong interest in mathematics and computing. The employment provides in-depth computer training and valuable hands-on experience which is rewarding financially and intellectually. Applicants should be expecting to gain a high grade at A-level maths. Positions are available in their London, Newbury and St Albans offices.

How to contact
To apply please contact Ruth Brennan at the address below in October/November preceding your A-level examinations

Address	Towers Perrin
	Castlewood House
	77-91 New Oxford Street
	London WC1A 1PX
Telephone	0171 379 4411
Fax	0171 379 7478/0532

FREETIME

PUBLICATIONS

AU PAIR & NANNY'S GUIDE TO WORKING ABROAD, THE

Covers opportunities to work overseas as a nanny or au pair

Whether you want to work abroad as a nanny, au pair or mother's help, this book covers: deciding to go, what training is necessary and finding work. Plus guides to 22 countries in Europe, North America and Australasia describing their advantages, regulations etc, and a directory of 200+ agencies.

Address	Vacation Work Publications
	9 Park End Street
	Oxford OX1 1HU
Telephone	01865 241 978
Fax	01865 790 885
Price	£8.99
ISBN	1 85458 168 6

DIRECTORY OF JOBS & CAREERS ABROAD

This is a guide to all kinds of work abroad from school leavers to professionals

This is a guide to all kinds of work abroad giving essential information on permanent career opportunities around the world for

FREETIME

people from school leavers to fully-qualified professionals. Lists the professions and trades in demand overseas and gives all the facts on careers abroad in Europe, Australia, New Zealand, the USA, Canada etc, for teachers, doctors, nurses, journalists, computer operators, engineers, secretaries and many more.

Address	Vacation Work Publications
	9 Park End Street
	Oxford OX1 1HU
Telephone	01865 241 978
Fax	01865 790 885
Price	£16.99
ISBN	1 85458 166 X

DIRECTORY OF SUMMER JOBS ABROAD, THE

A definitive guide to summer jobs abroad

This directory contains details of over 30,000 vacancies in over 50 countries from Andorra to Zaire for sports instructors, bar staff, holiday company reps, Kibbutz volunteers, English teachers, tour guides, farm hands, archaeologists, fruit pickers etc. Gives full details on the jobs offered including the period of work, what experience is required (if any) and wages (up to £1,000 per month) plus advice on work permits and health insurance, work with families and cheap travel. In May,

FREETIME

information received by Vacation Work too late for inclusion in *Summer Jobs Abroad* is published on 5 May in an up-to-date supplement available for an extra £6.

Address	Vacation Work Publications
	9 Park End Street
	Oxford OX1 1HU
Telephone	01865 241 978
Fax	01865 790 885
Price	£7.99
ISBN	1 85458 154 6

DIRECTORY OF SUMMER JOBS IN BRITAIN, THE

Lists over 30,000 vacancies in the UK

Work available includes fruit picking, hotel work, child care, holiday camps, archaeological digs, voluntary work etc, plus details of vacation traineeships giving on-the-job work experience. The jobs can pay as much as £300 per week. Details of wages and hours, conditions of work and qualifications required are given, together with names and addresses of whom to contact when applying. Plus advice on approaching an employer and creating your own job. In May, information received by Vacation Work too late for inclusion in *Summer Jobs In Britain* is published on 5 May in an up-to-date supplement available for an extra £6.

FREETIME

Address	Vacation Work Publications
	9 Park End Street
	Oxford OX1 1HU
Telephone	01865 241 978
Fax	01865 790 885
Price	£7.99
ISBN	1 85458 156 2

DIRECTORY OF VOLUNTEERING AND EMPLOYMENT OPPORTUNITIES

Guide to opportunities for both voluntary and paid work in Britain

This is a guide for both voluntary and paid work in Britain's major charities and voluntary organisations. It covers over 500 charities working in areas such as disability, housing and homelessness, social welfare and work with young people, and offers guidance on finding a suitable charity.

Address	The Directory of Social
	Change
	24 Stephenson Way
	London NW1 2DP
Telephone	0171 209 5151
Fax	0171 209 5049
Price	£9.95
ISBN	1 87386 071 4

FREETIME

DIRECTORY OF WORK & STUDY IN DEVELOPING COUNTRIES

A guide to employment, voluntary work and academic opportunities in the Third World

This is a guide to employment, voluntary work and academic opportunities in the Third World for those who wish to experience life there as more than a tourist. Thousands of short and long term opportunities for work and study with over 400 organisations in Africa, the Middle East, Asia, the Far East, the Pacific, Latin America and the Caribbean, including health care, engineering, disaster relief, agriculture, business, teaching, archaeology, economics, oil, irrigation etc.

Address	Vacation Work Publications
	9 Park End Street
	Oxford OX1 1HU
Telephone	01865 241 978
Fax	01865 790 885
Price	£8.99
ISBN	1 85458 170 8

FREETIME

EUROPE: THE LIVEWIRE GUIDE TO LIVING AND WORKING IN THE EC

A guide for the school leaver heading for work in Europe. It offers practical information on a range of areas including accommodation, employment and health services. Available through libraries, bookshops, or direct from the address below.

Address	Livewire Books
	The Women's Press
	34 Great Sutton Street
	London EC1V 0DX
Telephone	0171 251 3007
Fax	0171 608 1938
Price	£4.99
ISBN	0 70434 929 9

INTERNATIONAL DIRECTORY OF VOLUNTARY WORK

This book contains details of over 700 organisations that are looking for voluntary help from all types of people for all kinds of work. Covers short, medium and long term residential opportunities in Europe and around the world in addition to non-residential opportunities in the UK. Both skilled and unskilled people are needed, whether to help for a few hours or a few years work on a development project in Mozambique or help on a monkey sanctuary in Cornwall.

Address	Vacation Work Publications
	9 Park End Street
	Oxford OX1 1HU

Telephone	01865 241 978
Fax	01865 790 885
Price	£9.99
ISBN	1 85458 164 3

INTERNSHIPS 1997

Work experience for students and graduates in the USA

Internship is the American word for short term work experience that enables students and graduates to get invaluable on-the-job training for a future career. This book contains over 35,000 career-orientated internship positions in the USA, covering fields ranging from business to the theatre, communications to science. The majority of these opportunities are open to non-American students. This book explains when, where and how to apply for both positions and work permits.

Address	Vacation Work Publications
	9 Park End Street
	Oxford OX1 1HU
Telephone	01865 241 978
Fax	01865 790 885
Price	£15.99
ISBN	1 56079 645 6

FREETIME

KIBBUTZ VOLUNTEER

Comprehensive guide to Kibbutz life

This guide not only gives full details of 200 Kibbutzim and conveys their special atmosphere but also covers other short term work including the Moshav Movement, conservation, archaeological digs, fruit picking, au pair and hotel work etc.

Address	Vacation Work Publications
	9 Park End Street
	Oxford OX1 1HU
Telephone	01865 241 978
Fax	01865 790 885
Price	£7.99
ISBN	1 85458 142 2

SUMMER JOBS USA

Lists over 20,000 summer vacancies for students in the USA

From Alabama to Wyoming, there are lists of vacancies in summer theatres, on ranches, in National Parks and resorts and in theme and amusement parks with positions for sports instructors, camp staff, office workers, chamber staff etc. Summer Jobs USA gives information on wages (up to $450 a week), the duration of jobs, what qualifications, if any, the employer is looking for, etc, plus a special section providing advice on visa and other legal requirements for non-American applicants. Other features include the comments of employers on the attractions and advantages of particular jobs.

Address	Vacation Work Publications
	9 Park End Street
	Oxford OX1 1HU
Telephone	01865 241 978
Fax	01865 790 885
Price	£10.99
ISBN	1 56079 660 X

TEACHING ENGLISH ABROAD

Guide to short term and long term jobs teaching English overseas

This guide is for both trained and untrained teachers in the booming field of teaching English as a foreign language. Contains substantial chapters on over 25 countries where EFL is a major industry, including Spain, Korea, Greece, Poland, the Czech and Slovak Republics, Chile, Turkey, Japan and Thailand. Covers the ways in which English speakers can find work there and lists language schools which hire English teachers. Also surveys the possiblities in Africa and Latin America. Provides full information on

FREETIME

how to become qualified in EFL, the role of recruitment agencies and possible risks and how to avoid them.

Address	Vacation Work Publications
	9 Park End Street
	Oxford OX1 1HU
Telephone	01865 241 978
Fax	01865 790 885
Price	£9.99
ISBN	1 85458 160 0

TEENAGERS' VACATION GUIDE TO WORK, STUDY & ADVENTURE

This book covers the wide range of jobs, study courses and adventure holidays that are available in Britain and abroad for teenagers aged between 13 and 18 during the school vacations. Lists hundreds of employers, language schools and other educational establishments, adventure holidays etc.

Address	Vacation Work Publications
	9 Park End Street
	Oxford OX1 1HU
Telephone	01865 241 978
Fax	01865 790 885
Price	£6.95
ISBN	1 85458 044 2

FREETIME

WORK YOUR WAY AROUND THE WORLD

Working opportunities as you travel around the world

This guide is for the working traveller and incorporates hundreds of first-hand accounts and offers authoritative advice on how to find work around the world, either arranged in advance or found on the spot. It covers sections on working opportunities in places as diverse as Russia, Hawaii and South Africa and covers working a passsage, childcare jobs worldwide including Australia, fruit picking from Denmark to New Zealand, voluntary projects in Latin America and Africa etc. Also includes updated information on how to work a passage, dates and details of harvests around the world, how to become a barmaid, pineapple picker, ski tow operator, jackaroo, au pair, English teacher, camp counsellor etc.

Address	Vacation Work Publications
	9 Park End Street
	Oxford OX1 1HU
Telephone	01865 241 978
Fax	01865 790 885
Price	£10.99
ISBN	1 85458 162 7

FREETIME

WORKING IN SKI RESORTS – EUROPE & NORTH AMERICA

Guide for anyone who wants to find work as a ski instructor, disc jockey, ski technician, courier, chalet girl, shop assistant, office worker, au pair, resort rep, snow clearer etc. Plus reports on over 80 resorts in Europe and North America.

Address	Vacation Work Publications
	9 Park End Street
	Oxford OX1 1HU
Telephone	01865 241 978
Fax	01865 790 885
Price	£8.95
ISBN	1 85458 109 0

FREETIME

WORKING ON CRUISE SHIPS

Describes what over 150 jobs at sea are like and how to get them, including work as a social hostess, port lecturer, croupier, engineer, nurse, waiter, deck officer, gentleman host, hairdresser, entertainer, galley staff etc. Plus addresses of the agencies and cruise lines to apply to.

Address	Vacation Work Publications
	9 Park End Street
	Oxford OX1 1HU
Telephone	01865 241 978
Fax	01865 790 885
Price	£7.99
ISBN	1 85458 150 3

FREETIME

WEB SITES

BRITISH COUNCIL – HOW TO BECOME A TEACHER OF ENGLISH

Information on teaching English as a first language

Web site
http://www.britcoun.org/english/insteach.htm

OVERSEAS JOBS EXPRESS BOOKSHOP

Listing of books available to buy on-line about working holidays abroad

Web site
http://www.hiway.co.uk/expats/ojebk.html

FREETIME

HEALTH

ORGANISATIONS

ADULT DYSLEXIA ORGANISATION

Helpline

Helpline for people concerned with dyslexia. Also offers assistance to professional service providers. Provides information, help, advice, counselling and referrals.

Groups served
People concerned with dyslexia and service providers for people with dyslexia

Address	336 Brixton Road
	London SW9 7AA
Telephone	0171 924 9559
Fax	0171 207 7796

AIDS AHEAD

HIV advice for deaf people

London office of the British Deaf Association's Health Promotion Service offering HIV/AIDS information for deaf people. Provides information on accessing advice, support and counselling, befriending and specialist consultation for deaf people affected by HIV and related issues.

Groups served
Deaf and hard of hearing people

HEALTH

Address	British Deaf Association
	1-3 Worship Street
	London EC2A 2AB
Telephone	0171 588 3251
Fax	0171 588 3523
Minicom	0171 588 3530

ASIAN CANCER INFORMATION HELPLINE

Telephone service for Asian people who have or are caring for someone with cancer. Offers confidential information and support on any aspect of cancer in Hindi, Bengali, Urdu, Punjabi and English. Part of Cancerlink.

Address	11-21 Northdown Street
	London N1 9BN
Telephone	0800 590415 (freephone)
Fax	0171 833 4963
Minicom	0800 132905

AVMA – ACTION FOR VICTIMS OF MEDICAL ACCIDENTS

Advice and information for people who feel they have been a victim of a medical accident. Provides medical and legal advice and also runs a support network.

Groups served
General public

HEALTH

Address	Bank Chambers
	1 London Road
	Forest Hill
	London SE23 3TP
Telephone	0181 291 2793
Fax	0181 699 0632

BACUP

Cancer info/advice

National charity providing information and counselling for people affected by cancer. Information service is staffed by specialist nurses. Wide range of booklets available. Face-to-face counselling in London and Glasgow.

Groups served
People affected in any way by cancer

Address	3 Bath Place
	Rivington Street
	London EC2A 3JR
Telephone	0800 181199
	(Cancer info service)

BC AIDS HOMELINK SERVICE

Helpline

Helpline for Irish people affected by HIV living outside Northern Ireland and those who are considering returning. Information, advice and counselling relating to medical services, housing, employment, support agencies, emotional/social implications etc.

Groups served
Irish people affected by HIV

Address	Level 5, Outpatient Centre
	Royal Victoria Hospital
	Belfast BT12 6BA
Telephone	01232 439888
Fax	01232 245280

BRITISH DEAF ASSOCIATION HEALTH PROMOTION DEPARTMENT

Sex education/HIV/AIDS support

Provides advice, information, counselling and workshops about health and sexual health for deaf and hard of hearing people. Also supports hearing impaired people with HIV/AIDS, their partners and families and provides a buddy service. Counselling and workshops usually charged to local health authority or GP.

Groups served
Any deaf or hard of hearing person

HEALTH

Address	17 Macon Court
	Herald Drive
	Crewe
	Cheshire CW1 6EE
Telephone	01270 250736
Fax	01270 250742
Minicom	01270 250743

BRITISH EPILEPSY ASSOCIATION

Advice, information and support, including a telephone helpline for people with epilepsy. National network of self-help groups run education courses for lay and professional groups and promote research into the condition and its medical and social aspects.

Groups served
People with epilepsy, their families, friends, carers, partners, professionals

Address	Anstey House
	40 Hanover Square
	Leeds LS3 1BE
Telephone	0800 309 030 (helpline)
Fax	0113 242 8804

BRITISH INSTITUTE FOR BRAIN INJURED CHILDREN (BIBIC)

Therapy and support for parents of brain injured children. Provides training for parents on techniques of maximum sensory stimulation with the aim of encouraging the child's neurological development and progression. No child is refused a service due to the severity of his or her problem. Donations are requested towards the costs of treatment.

Groups served
Parents of brain injured children

Address	Knowle Hall
	Bridgwater
	Somerset TA7 8PJ
Telephone	01278 684060
Fax	01278 685573

CANCER AND LEUKAEMIA IN CHILDHOOD (CLIC)

CLIC nurses provide medical care and assistance at home. CLIC play therapists attend clinical sessions. Crisis-break flats in seaside towns provide free breaks. Homes near the specialist hospitals where children receive treatment provide free accommodation and individual grants to families in financial stress.

Groups served
Children (up to 21) suffering from cancer or leukaemia and their families

HEALTH

Address   12-13 King Square
               Bristol BS2 8JH
Telephone   0117 924 8844
Fax   0117 924 4505

CANCERLINK

Emotional support and information on all aspects of cancer. Acts as a resource for over 500 cancer support and self-help groups and individual supporters throughout the UK. Helps people set up new groups and offers training, development and consultancy. Produces a range of publications on practical and emotional issues.

Groups served
Anyone affected by cancer and their families, friends and involved professionals

Address   11-21 Northdown Street
            London N1 9BN
Telephone   0800 132 095 (freephone)
Fax   0171 833 4963
Minicom   0800 132 905

CARDIOMYOPATHY ASSOCIATION

Helpline

For sufferers of cardiomyopathy (any chronic disorder affecting the muscle of the heart). Also for families, health professionals and

HEALTH

other interested parties. Offers information and support relating to symptoms, medication etc. Information packs available.

Groups served
Sufferers of cardiomyopathy, their families, health professionals

Address	40 The Metro Centre
	Tolpits Lane
	Watford WD1 8SB
Telephone	01923 249977

CATHOLIC AIDS LINKS (CAL)

HIV/AIDS support

A Catholic-based group offering non-judgemental, spiritual, emotional, practical and financial support to anyone living with or affected by HIV/AIDS. Produces a newsletter and other publications. Has a limited hardship fund available. The telephone number is also the contact for Positively Catholic – a self-help support group which meets monthly.

Groups served
People living with or affected by HIV/AIDS, particularly in the Catholic community

Address	PO Box 201
	Winchester SO23 9XA
Telephone	0171 485 7298
Fax	01962 860221

HEALTH

CHILDHOOD CANCER HELPLINE

Helpline for anyone whose life has been affected by a child with cancer – children and adults. Offers a listening ear, providing callers with emotional support, befriending, telephone counselling, bereavement support, information.

Address	62 Walter Road
	Swansea SA1 4PT
Telephone	0800 30 30 31 (freephone)
Fax	01792 480700

CHILDREN'S LIVER DISEASE FOUNDATION

Information and education about children's liver disease for the general public and medical professionals. Offers emotional support to families with a child with liver disease. The foundation also funds research into all aspects of liver disease in children.

Groups served
General public and medical professionals

Address	138 Digbeth
	Birmingham B5 6DR
Telephone	0121 643 7282
Fax	0121 643 8262

DIAL UK – DISABLEMENT INFORMATION & ADVICE LINES

National organisation for the DIAL network of over 100 disability information and advice services. DIAL groups give free, independent advice on all aspects of disability and are run and staffed by people with direct experience of disability.

Groups served
People with physical disabilities
Address   St Catherine's Hospital
                          Tickhill Road
                          Balby
                          Doncaster DN4 8QN
Telephone   01302 310123
Fax   01302 310404
E-mail
dialuk@aol.com
Web site
http://members.aol.com/dialuk

DISABILITY SCOTLAND

Promoting equality of opportunity for people with disabilities in Scotland

Disability Scotland provides information and advice on disability issues and also publishes a number of directories on a wide range of topics relevant to disabled people from beds

HEALTH

and lifting aids to holidays and further education. Enquiry service open to young people who have any non-medical questions, relating to such things as access, the arts, further education and training, sport and leisure, grant making trusts and holidays. Disability Scotland is also carrying out a project to help disabled people and their carers to access services to which they are entitled under 'Community Care' legislation. Disability Scotland offers opportunities for volunteering in all aspects of its work, contact directly for information on current opportunities.

Address	Princes House
	5 Shandwick Place
	Edinburgh
	Scotland EH2 4RG
Telephone	0131 229 8632
Fax	0131 229 5168

HAEMOPHILIA SOCIETY

Advice on education, training, employment and all facets of life with haemophilia. Representation to local and central government on appropriate issues. Network of local groups hold meetings to discuss matters of common interest. Financial and other help.

HEALTH

Groups served

People with haemophilia, their families, partners and carers

Address   Chesterfield House
                   385 Euston Road
                   London NW1 3AU
Telephone   0171 380 0600
Fax   0171 387 8220

HIV COUNSELLING SERVICE

Helpline

Advice, information and support for people with concerns about HIV/AIDS. Access to pre- and post-test counselling and on-going counselling for people affected by HIV and AIDS. Also provides face-to-face counselling. Part of Forest Healthcare NHS Trust. Appointments available early morning and evening by arrangement.

Address   60 St Mary Road
                   Walthamstow
                   London E17 9RE
Telephone   0181 520 3766
Fax   0181 509 3920

HEALTH

INSTITUTE FOR COMPLEMENTARY MEDICINE

Provides information on complementary medicine and practitioners throughout the UK. Encourages research on the safety and effectiveness of complementary medicines. Produces a directory of practitioners.

Groups served
General public

Address	PO Box 194
	London SE16 1QZ
Telephone	0171 237 5165
Fax	0171 237 5175

INTERNATIONAL GLAUCOMA ASSOCIATION

Helpline

Telephone service for glaucoma sufferers and their relatives. Offers information, advice, reassurance and listening. Also supplies information booklets and leaflets free of charge.

Groups served
Glaucoma sufferers and their relatives

HEALTH

Address	c/o Kings College Hospital
	Denmark Hill
	London SE5 9RS
Telephone	0171 737 3265
Fax	0171 346 5929

MAC HELPLINE FOR YOUNG PEOPLE AFFECTED BY CANCER

Information and support for young people affected by cancer on issues such as screening, diagnosis, physical and emotional aspects of cancer, medical treatments, complementary therapies, risk reduction, local cancer services. Part of Cancerlink.

Groups served
Young people affected by cancer

Address	11-21 Northdown Street
	London N1 9BN
Telephone	0800 591 028 (freephone)

MEN'S HEALTH LINE

Telephone health and information service on issues relating to men's health eg, genetic disorders, prostate problems, cardiac problems, impotence, STDs, sports injuries, etc. Staffed by fully qualified nurses. The aim is not to replace a doctor's advice but to complement it and to ensure that the patient knows the correct course of action.

HEALTH

Groups served
General public wanting information on men's
health issues

Address   Medical Advisory Service
PO Box 3087
London W4 4ZP

Telephone   0181 995 4448

MIND (NATIONAL ASSOCIATION FOR MENTAL HEALTH)

Administrative HQ with 200 local
associations. Campaigns for good quality
local mental health services, offers training,
community development advice and
advocacy services, including a legal service.
Publishes a range of books, leaflets etc.

Groups served
People with mental health problems, their
carers, families etc. General public

Address   Granta House
15-19 Broadway, Stratford
London E15 4BQ

Telephone   0181 519 2122

MULTIPLE SCLEROSIS SOCIETY

National organisation with 400 local
branches. Promotes and encourages research
into MS. Provides welfare and support

HEALTH

services including: counselling for the newly diagnosed; financial support and advice/information. Publications list available – send a large SAE.

Groups served
Anyone affected by multiple sclerosis
Address   25 Effie Road
                 London SW6 1EE
Telephone   0171 371 8000 (helpline)
Fax   0171 736 9861

NATIONAL AIDS HELPLINE

Information, advice and counselling on all aspects of HIV/AIDS and sexual health. Can also provide specific literature and referrals to specialist services. Advice in the following languages: Cantonese, Punjabi, Bengali, Gujarati, Urdu, Hindi, Arabic and Welsh – phone for times and phone numbers for these services.

Groups served
General public
Address   PO Box 5000
                 Glasgow G12 8BR
Telephone   0800 567 123
                 (24-hour helpline)
Fax   0141 334 0299
Minicom   0800 521 361
                 (textphone 10am-10pm)

HEALTH

NATIONAL BACK PAIN ASSOCIATION

Advice and information for back and neck pain sufferers. Carries out educative work and has local branches.

Address	16 Elmtree Road Teddington Middlesex TW11 8ST
Telephone	0181 977 5474
Fax	0181 943 5318

NATIONAL DEAF CHILDREN'S SOCIETY

Advice on the education and welfare of deaf children. Information service for parents, professionals and the general public. Offers training and consultancy and information on equipment and technology.

Groups served
Deaf children, their parents/carers and professionals working with them

Address	15 Dufferin Street London EC1Y 8PD
Telephone	0171 250 0123
Fax	0171 251 5020
Minicom	0171 250 0123

NATIONAL DEAF CHILDREN'S SOCIETY FAMILY FREEPHONE

Info/advice for deaf children/young people and their families. Areas covered include: education, benefits, local and national services. Support for families experiencing problems coping with their situation, putting families in contact with each other.

Groups served
Deaf children/young people and their families
Address   15 Dufferin Street
                      London EC1Y 8PD
Telephone   0800 252 380 (freephone)

NATIONAL KIDNEY FEDERATION

Advice and information centre for patients and families and is the central office for the federation which has 52 member associations in Scotland, England and Wales. Produces leaflets and a magazine. Association activities include purchase of medical equipment, holiday facilities. All run by kidney patients, they represent the interests of patients and campaign to increase treatment facilities.

Groups served
Patients, families, members of the public

HEALTH

Address	6 Stanley Street
	Worksop S81 7HX
Telephone	01909 487795
Fax	01909 487123

NATIONAL SOCIETY FOR EPILEPSY

Provides assessment, treatment, rehabilitation, long term care and respite care for adults with epilepsy. Information and education department produces educational resources and runs a national helpline (01494 601 400). Community network of support groups.

Groups served
Adults with epilepsy and their families/carers

Address	Chalfont St Peter
	Gerrards Cross
	Bucks SL9 0RJ
Telephone	01494 601 300/601 400
	(helpline)
Fax	01494 871 927

RATHBONE CI (COMMUNITY INDUSTRY)

Learning difficulties helpline

HQ of a charity working across the UK for people with moderate learning difficulties or who have special educational or training needs. Runs a Learning Difficulties Helpline offering advice and information to people with learning difficulties, parents, carers and professionals. Also provides services including training and employment, residential and independent living centres.

Groups served
People with learning difficulties, parents, carers and professionals

Address	1st Floor
	The Excalibur Building
	77 Whitworth Street
	Manchester M1 6EZ
Telephone	0161 236 1877 (helpline)
Fax	0161 236 4539

RESCARE

Learning disability advice

The National Society for Mentally Handicapped People in residential care. Provides advice and support to individuals with learning disabilities and their families, including those who are cared for in the family home. Also campaigns to promote choice of residential care options.

Groups served
Children and adults with learning disabilities and their families

HEALTH

Address	Rayner House
	23 Higher Hillgate
	Stockport
	Cheshire SK1 3ER
Telephone	0161 474 7372
Fax	0161 480 3668

ROYAL NATIONAL INSTITUTE FOR THE BLIND (RNIB) – CUSTOMER SERVICE CENTRE

Advice and information for people with visual impairment/sight loss that inhibits daily living, families and carers. Offers advice on benefits, publications on daily living, talking book service and sells adapted aids and gadgets. Also advises organisations on how to make services accessible to blind or partially-sighted people.

Groups served
People with visual impairment

Address	PO Box 173
	Peterborough
	Cambs PE2 6WS
Telephone	0345 023153
Fax	01733 391865

SCOPE

Range of services for people with cerebral palsy, including schools, colleges, residential care, information and careers advice. Free helpline. A network of local teams across England and Wales provides contact with social workers and over 200 local groups. Please note SCOPE is due to move to Highland House, Market Road, London in December 1997.

Groups served
People with cerebral palsy and their families/carers
Address   12 Park Crescent
                London W1N 4EQ
Telephone   0800 626 216 (helpline)
Fax   0171 436 2601

SENSE – THE NATIONAL DEAFBLIND & RUBELLA ASSOCIATION

Campaigns for the needs of deafblind children and young adults. Provides advice, support and services including educational advice, self-help groups, residential and respite care, publications and an 'usher' service.

Groups served
Deafblind people, their families/carers and professional staff working with them

HEALTH

Address	11-13 Clifton Terrace
	London N4 3SR
Telephone	0171 272 7774
Fax	0171 272 6012
Minicom	0171 272 9648

SOFT UK (SUPPORT ORGANISATION FOR TRISOMY 13)

Part of SOFT UK – Support Organisation for Trisomy 13/18 and Related Disorders, this one being the support group for Trisomy 13 (Patau's Syndrome). Offers links to other members, parental befriending, bereavement support, loan of videos and information pack (free for parents, £3 for professionals). Provides specialist feeders. A professional representative is available to liaise with medics.

Groups served
Parents/relatives, health care workers of babies/children with the disorder

Address	Tudor Lodge
	Redwood
	Ross on Wye HR9 5UD
Telephone	01989 567480

HEALTH

SPOD

Telephone helpline

Telephone counselling for disabled people, their partners or carers to discuss issues of sexuality or relationships. Also produces publications. SPOD stands for Sexual and Personal Relationships of People with a Disability.

Groups served
Disabled people
Address   286 Camden Road
                   London N7 0BJ
Telephone   0171 607 8851

TERRENCE HIGGINS TRUST

Services for people affected by HIV/AIDS including: advice and information (welfare rights, legal services and housing); counselling and support, buddying and practical help. Helpline open 365 days a year (12 noon-10pm). Legal line 0171 405 2381 (7pm-10pm Monday and Wednesday) for legal advice on HIV/AIDS issues. Health promotion work and campaigning.

Groups served
Anyone affected by HIV/AIDS

HEALTH

Address	52-54 Grays Inn Road
	London WC1X 8JU
Telephone	0171 242 1010
	(helpline 12 noon-10pm)
Fax	0171 242 0121

WEB SITES

ABILITY

Information directory of health issues, including special needs

Web site
http://www.ability.org.uk

AMERICAN BRAIN TUMOR ASSOCIATION

The latest treatments, information and help on brain tumors

Web site
http://www.abta.org

MENTAL HEALTH NET

Comprehensive guide to mental health on-line

Web site
http://www.cmhc.com

HEALTH

HOUSING

SITE

ORGANISATIONS

CHAS HOUSING AID (LONDONWIDE AND NATIONAL OFFICE)

Telephone advice on all aspects of housing, especially homelessness. (For people with more complex problems who have telephoned first, face-to-face appointments may be made.) This is also the national office of CHAS which runs nine advice centres in England. Provides an education programme and publishes education packs, reports, briefings and other information on homelessness.

Groups served
Anyone needing advice on housing problems or homelessness. NB visitors to office by appointment only

Address	209 Old Marylebone Road London NW1 5QT
Telephone	0171 723 5928 (advice)
Fax	0171 723 5943

CENTREPOINT

Provides housing for young, single, homeless people in a variety of projects

Centrepoint provides a range of different accommodation to which young people

HOUSING

between the ages of 16 and 25 can be referred, usually by other agencies operating in the West End of London. Young people can refer themselves to Centrepoint's nightshelters.

Other projects Centrepoint provides are:

Hostels for young women – Camden

Three Foyers – accommodation/training and work placement

A high-support project for young people who are not able to live independently at the moment (Buffy House)

A housing team that works like a housing association for independent young people and a safe house for young runaways under 16 years

Address	Bewlay House
	2 Swallow Place
	London W1R 7AA
Telephone	0171 629 2229
Fax	0171 409 2027

HOUSING

FOYER FEDERATION FOR YOUTH

Support for young people who are homeless or in housing need and/or unemployed

Foyers are hostels which offer affordable accommodation, access to skills training, support and job hunting advice all under one roof. They are aimed at young people aged between 16 and 25 who are unemployed, homeless or starting out on a new career. Foyers aim to help young people avoid the 'no-job-no-home' trap and will provide young people with accommodation, help and support for up to two years. There are now almost 30 Foyers across the UK with another 30 under development. The Foyer Federation is the national agency which coordinates the Foyer network and helps promote the development of new Foyers – Foyers are run locally by voluntary agencies and housing associations. Please see the organisations local to you for details of their individual services.

Address	2nd Floor, Humatt House
	146-148 Clerkenwell Road
	London EC1R 5DP
Telephone	0171 833 8616
Fax	0171 833 8717
E-mail	
federation@foyer.net	
Web site	
http://www.foyer.net	

PRIORITY YOUTH HOUSING

Provider of accommodation for 16-25-year-olds in Bristol

Priority provides affordable accommodation with support to single young homeless people aged between 16 and 25 years old in Bristol.

Address	Priority Youth Housing
	62 Bedminster Parade
	Bristol BS3 4HL
Telephone	0117 953 0404
Fax	0117 923 1404
E-mail	

priority@gn.apc.org

SALVATION ARMY – LONDON OUTREACH TEAM

Outreach work on the streets in the evenings with people sleeping rough. Offers housing advice sessions 10am-1pm and general advice 1-4pm. Also provides resettlement service and support. Food available on Wednesday evenings. Access to drug, alcohol and mental health services.

Groups served
Homeless people sleeping out on the streets

HOUSING

Address	97 Rochester Row
	London SW1P 1JL
Telephone	0171 233 9862
Fax	0171 613 4412

SHELTER – LONDON LINE

Free telephone housing advice service offering help and advice on any housing problem, including homelessness, harassment and eviction. Calls are directed to the appropriate team within Shelter, or referred to local agencies. Emergency hostel referrals.

Groups served
People who are homeless or those with a housing problem

Address	88 Old Street
	London EC1V 9HU
Telephone	0800 446 441
Minicom	0800 622 410

SHELTER – LONDON

An organisation to help the homeless find homes

SHELTER is a registered charity, which offers free advice and assistance on finding housing. SHELTER also provides the advocacy to help solve a wide range of housing problems.

Address	88 Old Street
	London EC1V 9HU
Telephone	0171 505 2000
Fax	0171 505 2169

E-mail
100065.347@compuserve.com

YOUNG MEN'S CHRISTIAN ASSOCIATION (YMCA)

The YMCA provides a range of services and activities, including housing for the homeless, vocational training, recreation, sporting activities, drug and alcohol counselling and advice, and much more. There are over 150 YMCAs across the UK and they are open to all.

Age range
The emphasis is on young people but anyone is welcome

Numbers passing through
One million each year in England

How to contact
Check telephone directory or contact the National Council for your nearest centre and contact direct for details of services available

Costs/waiting lists
Small charge for some activities; charges for membership and accommodation vary from association to association

HOUSING

Address	YMCA Regional Office
	50 Pitsford Drive
	Loughborough
	Leicestershire LE11 4NY
Telephone	01509 232752
Fax	01509 610822

E-mail
101526,2245@compuserve.com
Web site
http://www.ymca.org.uk

YWCA

Helps homeless women

Helps young women who are homeless find housing for long or short terms.

Address	Headquarters and Registered
	Office
	Claredon House
	52 Cornmarket Street
	Oxford OX1 3EJ
Telephone	01865 736 110
Fax	01865 204 805

HOUSING

SEX

ORGANISATIONS

ABORTION LAW REFORM ASSOCIATION

ALRA campaigns for a woman's right to choose on abortion, in law and in practice

Provides practical and legal information on unwanted pregnancy and abortion. ALRA will also supply educational information for projects, debates, essays etc.

Address   11-13 Charlotte Street
            London W1P 1HD
Telephone   0171 637 7264

BISEXUAL HELPLINE

Telephone counselling, listening and information for anyone with concerns regarding bisexuality. Issues dealt with include relationships, personal life crises, HIV prevention, local bisexual groups etc. Referrals for face-to-face counselling.

Groups served
Anyone with concerns regarding bisexuality
Address   PO Box 3325
            London N1 9EQ
Telephone   0181 569 7500

THE BOOK

BRITISH PREGNANCY ADVISORY SERVICE

Central office for BPAS running a helpline and
30 consultation centres offering information,
counselling and treatments linked with
unplanned pregnancy and fertility control.
Also offers pregnancy testing, advice on
contraceptives, emergency contraception,
abortion, sterilisation, vasectomy, after-
abortion support. In parts of the country BPAS
is able to provide free help, otherwise charges
are kept to a minimum.

Groups served
General public
Address   Austy Manor
                     Wooten Wawen
                     Solihull B95 6BX
Telephone   0345 304030
Fax   01564 794935

BROOK – TOTTENHAM COURT ROAD

Sexual health/birth control

Free confidential information, advice and
counselling on contraception, pregnancy and
safer sex. Pregnancy tests (except for non-
clients over 20); follow-up care and
emergency contraception, psychosexual
counselling. Donations are requested for
women aged between 18 and 20 (£6 per

year), fees for women wanting birth control aged between 21 and 30 (£14 a visit or £35 per year). One of 14 centres across London.

Groups served
Young people under 21 and women up to 30 requiring emergency contraception

Address	233 Tottenham Court Road London W1P 9AE
Telephone	0171 580 2991 (appointments)

CHILDWATCH

Support around childhood abuse

Volunteer-run service offering telephone and face-to-face counselling for adults who have been abused as children and their families. Prevention work including talks/advice on child safety, leaflets and booklets on help for victims of child sexual abuse. Runs a shop to raise funds.

Groups served
Adults who have been abused as children and their families

Address	206 Hessle Road Hull HU3 3BE
Telephone	01482 325552
Fax	01482 585214

GAY AND LESBIAN LEGAL ADVICE (GLAD)

Telephone legal advice service on all aspects of the law for lesbians and gay men.

Address   Room H2
                   10-14 Macklin Street
                   London WC2B 5NF
Telephone   0171 831 3535

GAYLINE

Phoneline run by gay and bisexual students for other students (university and local FE colleges) and anyone else with gay-related problems. Offers a non-judgemental listening ear, some befriending and information on places to go locally. The line is always staffed by one man and one woman.

Address   Student Union
                   University of East Anglia
                   Norwich NR4 7TJ
Telephone   01603 592 505

SEX

GEMMA (LESBIANS WITH/WITHOUT DISABILITIES)

Gemma is a national self-help group of lesbians and bisexual women with/without disabilities which aims to lessen the isolation of disabled lesbians. Friendship, help with transport and general support. Quarterly newsletter.

Address   PO Box 5700
London WC1N 3XX

REACH (RAPE, EXAMINATION, ADVICE, COUNSELLING, HELP)

Support, counselling and advice to women who have been raped or sexually assaulted whether or not a formal complaint has been made to the police. Also offers access to a woman doctor for a full forensic medical examination and access to a woman police officer for advice and information. Counsellors available: Mon/Thu 10am-8pm, Wed 10am-12 noon and 3pm-8pm, Fri 10am-6pm.

Groups served
Women (16+) who have been raped or sexually assaulted

Address	Rhona Cross Centre
	Grainger Park Road
	Newcastle Upon Tyne
	NE4 8RQ
Telephone	0191 226 0825
Fax	0191 272 2485
Minicom	0191 272 0844

SEXWISE

Helpline

Information, advice and guidance for young people aged between 12 and 18 on various matters concerning sexuality and sexual health. Issues dealt with include: contraception, peer pressure, pregnancy, family planning clinics, STDs, feelings, emotions, relationships etc.

SEX

Address	PO Box 5000
	Glasgow G12 8BR
Telephone	0800 282 930 (freephone)
Fax	0141 334 0299

VICTIM SUPPORT (NATIONAL OFFICE)

Trained volunteers based in 378 local schemes offer emotional support, information and practical assistance to victims of crime, witnesses and their families. Witness services operate in all Crown Court centres in England and Wales.

Groups served
Victims of crime and witnesses of crime and their families

Address	Cranmer House
	39 Brixton Road
	London SW9 6DZ
Telephone	0171 735 9166
Fax	0171 582 5712

SEX

WOMEN'S AID FEDERATION ENGLAND

Telephone helpline for women experiencing physical, emotional or sexual violence in the home. Can refer callers to emergency and temporary accommodation and provide advice, information and support. All calls charged at local rates.

Groups served
Women and their children experiencing domestic violence

Address	PO Box 391
	Bristol BS99 7WS
Telephone	0345 023 468 (helpline)
Fax	0117 924 1703

SEX

THE BOOK

WEB SITES

AIDS NEWS FROM THE UK

Provides information on the AIDS epidemic in the UK

Web site
http://www.oneworld.org/avert/

CLINIC 275

A service that provides information on sexual health for students

Web site
http://www.eastend.com.au/clinic275/

GAY TO Z, THE

The UK's gay and lesbian directory

Web site
http://www.freedom.co.uk/gaytoz@

SEXUAL HEALTH

Informational service focused on sexual health

Web site
http://www.sexualhealth.com

SEX

WORK in SITE

ORGANISATIONS

ASSOCIATION OF CERTIFIED CHARTERED ACCOUNTANTS (ACCA)

Certified accountants may work in any of the three main fields of accountancy – public practice (accounting firms offering a range of accounting services), industry and commerce or the public sector (local or central government, or in publicly-owned industries). Contact them for careers and courses information and advice. ACCA not only serves England, Wales and Northern Ireland, but also has branches in Scotland, Dublin, Malaysia, Singapore, Hong Kong and South Africa.

Address   Student Recruitment and
                 Training
                 29 Lincoln's Inn Fields
                 London WC2A 3EE
Telephone   0171 396 5800
Fax   0171 396 5858
E-mail
student.recruitment@acca.co.uk
Web site
http://www.acca.co.uk

BUSINESS LINKS

Provide advice, information, and support for people starting their own business. The extensive Business Link network is the gateway to a comprehensive range of business support opportunities, services and information. Business Links help businesses compete, develop and grow in an increasingly competitive world marketplace. By bringing together all the support services available to businesses, Business Links provide the kind of quality help that really counts; how to raise money for growth; how to get into export markets; how to source the most suitable training packages; and how to manage change and help with the full range of issues affecting business. Business Links are open to all businesses great and small and are run by private sector-led partnerships of Training and Enterprise Councils, Chambers of Commerce, Enterprise Agencies, Local Authorities, government and other providers of business support. They're staffed by dedicated teams of advisers and specialists committed to help you succeed.

WORK

WORK

Address	103 New Oxford Street
	London WC1A 1DP
Telephone	0171 316 1000
Fax	0171 316 1001
Web site	

http://www.businesslink.co.uk

CAREERS SERVICES

Give general career advice

Career offices differ around the country in which services they provide to people. Depending on which company is in charge of your area, the advice may be free to everyone or restricted to certain groups of people.

However, no matter who you are, these offices will be able to give you general career advice and guidance.

CHARTERED INSTITUTE OF MARKETING (CIM)

Marketing covers a wide range of occupations, including brand management, market research, distribution/retail-selling, exporting and communications. The necessary knowledge/understanding for these roles can be gained by studying for the Institute's professional qualifications, including the internationally-recognised

Graduate Diploma in Marketing. The Institute is also an Awarding Body for N/SVQs in sales or, marketing. The principal aim of the Chartered Institute of Marketing is to establish marketing as a universally-recognised, understood and accepted profession reflecting the levels of quality standards and principles expected of a chartered body. The Institute offers many services including: training in marketing, sales, and strategy through open residential courses, seminars and company-specific programmes; consultancy services for marketing-related assignments in all market sectors worldwide; professional qualifications include the internationally-recognised Postgraduate Diploma of Marketing; vocational qualifications in sales, marketing, customer service and account management. CIM Information and Library service is available to members, student members and non-members; membership – members benefit from a wide range of services and facilities and belong to a regional Branch or Industry Group; CIM Direct, the Institute's publications sales service.

Address   Moor Hall
                   Cookham
                   Maidenhead
                   Berkshire SL6 9QH

WORK

Telephone   01628 427 500
Fax   01628 427 499
E-mail
marketing@cim.co.uk
Web site
http://www.cim.co.uk

CITY CENTRE

Advice for office workers

Information and advice to office workers on employment rights, health and safety including VDUs, race and sex discrimination and harassment. Also run workshops, publish literature, run seminars and provide training.

Groups served
Office workers
Address   32-35 Featherstone Street
    London EC1Y 8QX
Telephone   0171 608 1338

CIVIL AVIATION AUTHORITY (CAA)

Provides information on a career in aviation

The Civil Aviation Authority is a public authority outside the Civil Service. Among its functions is responsibility for National Air Traffic Services, 1,500 of whose 6,000 staff are air traffic controllers (ATCOs). They play a key role in the promotion of safe, regular, and expeditious flow of air traffic. If you become an ATCO you would have the chance to say where you would like to work, but you could be posted to any of the available units, depending on the vacancies when you graduate.

Address	Room t820
	CAA House
	45-49 Kingsway
	London WC2B 6TE
Telephone	0171 832 6651
	0171 832 5412

WORK

EMPLOYMENT SERVICE JOBCENTRE

Combined Unemployment Benefit Office and Jobcentre

Jobcentres are there to help people get work. Jobcentres have details of jobs employers want to fill. They will give advice and help on how to find work. Jobcentres also administer Unemployment Benefit and Income Support.

Address	Westminster ESJ
	Chadwick Street
	London SW1P2ES
Telephone	0171 853 3800
Fax	0171 853 3886

WORK

INSTANT MUSCLE LTD (IM)

Offers training and support to get a job or set up your own business

Instant Muscle is committed to helping unemployed people who face disadvantage or discrimination in the labour market to take up the challenge of running their own small business, or find a satisfying job. IM offers a wide variety of training courses and one-to-one counselling from 35 centres across England and Wales. Applicants should be unemployed and in receipt of benefit.

How to contact
Through Head Office, who will refer you to a centre near you
Costs/waiting lists
All services are free. Waiting lists vary between regions – in some, opportunities are almost immediately available

Address	Springside House
	84 North End Road
	London W14 9ES
Telephone	0171 603 2604
Fax	0171 603 7346
E-mail	

Instant_Muscle_HO@MSN.COM

INSTITUTE OF TRAVEL AND TOURISM
(ITT)

The professional body for the travel and tourism industry

The institute accredits college courses, our approved courses in travel and tourism assure students of the highest quality education and preparation for a career in the travel industry. Essential reading for anyone who is interested in a career in tourism is the Institute's guide to careers and courses in travel and tourism.

Address	113 Victoria Street
	St Albans
	Hertfordshire AL1 3TJ
Telephone	01727 854395
Fax	01727 847415
E-mail	

itt@dial.pipex.com

LECS – LOCAL ENTERPRISE COMPANIES
SCOTLAND

The Local Enterprise Companies in Scotland administer the government's training and employment initiatives. They will give information and advice on training in general and on such schemes as 'Skillseekers and Modern Apprenticeships', 'Work Experience for Graduates with Mentors', 'Graduates into

WORK

Business', 'Business Set-up Courses', 'Grants for Business and Economic Development'. Some of these schemes have qualifying criteria attached ie, applicants have to have been unemployed for a certain length of time or be within a specific age range. For full information and advice contact your LEC

Address	Scottish Enterprise
	120 Bothwell Street
	Glasgow G2 7JP
Telephone	0141 248 2700
Fax	0141 228 2511

E-mail
xxxx@scotent.co.uk
Web site
http://www.scotent.co.uk

LEDU: THE SMALL BUSINESS AGENCY

Helps small businesses in manufacturing and service activities

LEDU, the Small Business Agency for Northern Ireland, is the lead agency for local economic development in Northern Ireland which aims to encourage small businesses to grow and become more competitive. LEDU's headquarters are in Belfast and there are six regional offices throughout Northern Ireland, all of which can provide information and support in areas such as finance, product development, marketing and counselling. LEDU can provide a full range of services for anyone who is considering starting a business, or who has recently started a business or who wants to expand their business. Contact numbers for the six regional offices are available from the number below.

Address	Upper Galwally
	Belfast
	Northern Ireland BT8 4TB
Telephone	01232 491031
Fax	01232 691432
E-mail	

ledu@nics.gov.uk

WORK

LIVEWIRE

Provides information and support for setting up your own business

LiveWIRE can provide information, advice and support to young people who are thinking of starting their own business, and to those already established in business. Their free booklet *Could this be you?* is available to those wanting to start up their own business. LiveWIRE can also put you in touch with a local business adviser to help you develop your ideas and begin planning your business. A Business Opportunity Profile factsheet explains what is involved in setting up a

WORK

specific business idea, including the market potential, typical start-up costs and legal requirements. The LiveWIRE Business Start Up Awards offer over £190,000 cash awards and help in kind support. The competition is open to owner managers in their first year of trading, the awards are made by independent judging panels on the basis of the viability and potential of their business plan submission. The closing date for business plan submissions and completed entry forms to the local LiveWIRE coordinator is 31 January. The LiveWIRE Business Growth Challenge supports the owner managers to develop the skills required to manage a growing business. The LiveWIRE Export Challenge provides specialist export training and advice, including organised trade visits to Europe. The programme enables businesses to develop an export strategy, and facilitates entry to overseas markets.

Address	Hawthorne House
	Forth Banks
	Newcastle-upon-Tyne
	NE1 3SG
Telephone	0191 261 5584
E-mail	

livewire@projectne.co.uk

LOCAL GOVERNMENT OPPORTUNITIES

Provides information on opportunities to work in local government

Local government is not only big business it is one of the most diverse employers in England and Wales. At whatever level of entry you wish to join, local government may have an opportunity for you. Professional posts exist, for instance, architects and solicitors; specialists who train in a specific area such as environmental impact assessors; and administration staff who work directly with these others ensuring the smooth running of the operation. LGO can give information on the opportunities that exist in this increasingly competitive environment.

Address	Local Government Management Board 76-86 Turnmill Street London EC1M 5QU
Telephone	0171 296 6600
Fax	0171 296 6666
Web site	

http://www.datalake.com/lgo

WORK

WORK

NATIONAL COACHING FOUNDATION (NCF)

The NCF provides an education service for coaches. It offers a programme of coaching courses throughout the UK to meet the needs of coaches of all sports and all levels of experience. If you would like information on the NCF's services, details of courses in your area, contact addresses or advice on a career in coaching, write to us enclosing a large SAE (for 80p).

Regional addresses
The NCF has ten regional offices in England and works in partnership with the Scottish Coaching Unit, the Welsh National Coaching Centre and the Northern Ireland Institute of Coaching. Addresses and telephone numbers are available on request

Age range
Any

Address   114 Cardigan Road
Headingley
Leeds LS6 3BJ

Telephone   0113 2744802

NATIONAL SOCIETY FOR EDUCATION IN ART AND DESIGN (NSEAD)

Provides information on careers in art and design

The National Society for Education in Art and Design (NSEAD) is able to provide limited advice and contacts for those seeking a career in art and design. They publish *Creative Futures* which is a guide to courses and careers in art, craft and design, by Tony Charlton. It costs £12.30 including p&p.

Address	The Gatehouse
	Corsham Court
	Corsham
	Wiltshire SN13 0BZ
Telephone	01249 714 825
Fax	01249 716 138
E-mail	

100436.3041@compuserve.com

WORK

OPPORTUNITIES FOR PEOPLE WITH DISABILITIES (HQ)

Assists people with a wide range of disabilities to secure meaningful employment. Aims to persuade employers to recognise ability and potential, not disability and prejudice. Runs network of 13 regional centres and two job clubs providing

WORK

information, advice and help with training and job searches. Services are provided free to employers and disabled job seekers.

Groups served
People with disabilities

Address	1 Bank Buildings
	Princes Street
	London EC2R 8EU
Telephone	0171 726 4961
Fax	0171 7264961
Minicom	0171 726 4963

PACT

PACT provides comprehensive employment advice for people with disabilities

PACT's aim is to provide comprehensive employment advice and assessment for people with disabilities. PACT offers many services which are briefly described below. Disability Employment Advisers (DEAs) are located in jobcentres, their main priority is to give advice and guidance to disabled jobseekers and help them into work. Access to Work Scheme (ATW) is a programme funded by the Employment Service to give financial help in the provision of equipment and support to enable disabled employees to work on equal terms with their non-disabled colleagues. Client Matching Service where they hold the CVs of job-ready disabled people who are looking to work in the area and match them against vacancies suited to them.

Address	6th Floor
	19-29 Woburn Place
	London WC1H OLU
Telephone	0171 713 7911
Fax	0171 713 7920

WORK

PRINCE'S SCOTTISH YOUTH BUSINESS TRUST (PSYBT)

Provides loans, grants and advice to would-be entrepreneurs in Scotland

The aim of the Prince's Scottish Youth Business Trust is to provide seedcorn finance and professional support to young people in Scotland, aged between 18 and 25, whoever they are and wherever they come from, so that they can set up and continue to run their own businesses. The Trust has particular concern for the disadvantaged. Applicants must have a viable business idea, be unable to raise all or part of the finance necessary to set up their own business and be able to work at their business full time. The Trust offers free professional advice; access to pre-start training; loans of up to £5,000 over a period of up to five years at 4% interest; grants of up to £1,000; assistance from professional advisers once the applicant has started trading for a minimum period of two years.

Regional addresses
18+ regional managers – details available from Head Office

Numbers passing through
460 businesses were set up in the 1990-91 financial year, 437 in 1991-92, 411 in 1992-93, 367 in 1993-94 and 406 in 1994-95

How to contact
Contact nearest regional manager through one of the 44 Enterprise Trusts throughout Scotland

Costs/waiting lists
There are no waiting lists but it normally takes 12 weeks or more to prepare an application/business plan and complete the necessary training before the application is ready to be processed

Address	6th Floor
	Mercantile Chambers
	53 Bothwell Street
	Glasgow G2 6TS
Telephone	0141 248 4999
Fax	0141 248 4836

PRINCE'S TRUST – ACTION, THE

Helping people achieve their potential via training courses and grants

The Prince's Trust – Action helps young people facing problems like poverty, unemployment, discrimination, underachievement, family breakdown, homelessness and personal crisis. It achieves this through a range of dynamic programmes. Training – residential courses including 'Recharge' bringing together long term unemployed 18-25-year-olds and offering them a range of workshops in job-finding, social and vocational skills. 'Superstart' is for 16-17-year-olds 'at risk'. 'Rock School' aims to help develop confidence through music and a series of local training initiatives catering to local needs. Grants – Prince's Trust – Action provides grants to individuals for projects that will have a direct impact on their lives. European Link – provides opportunities to make links with counterparts in other European countries. 'Go and See, Go and Help' grants enable you to explore projects, exchange ideas or to take part in voluntary work.

WORK

WORK

Address	18 Park Square East
	London NW1 4LH
Telephone	0800 842 842
Fax	0171 543 1200

E-mail
printrust@princes-trust.org.uk
Web site
http://www.princes-trust.org.uk

PRINCE'S YOUTH BUSINESS TRUST

Provides loans, grants and advice to would-be entrepreneurs

PYBT helps people to start their own business. They must be disadvantaged eg, through unemployment, family circumstances, lack of education, and be unable to raise all the money they need elsewhere. Loans up to £5,000 on easy repayment terms and grants up to £1,500 are awarded to people with a good business idea but without adequate means to finance it. In addition to finance PYBT provides each supported business with a volunteer Business Adviser and directs clients to suitable enterprise training.

Age range
18-30
Numbers passing through
Approximately 25,000 enquiries each year leading to about 4,000 people receiving

grants or loans
How to contact
For general information call the freephone number 0800 842 842
Costs/waiting lists
There are no costs to the applicant in applying and no waiting list. All proposals are evaluated on their individual merits

Address	18 Park Square East
	London NW1 4LH
Telephone	0171 543 1234
Fax	0171 543 1258

E-mail
printrust@princes-trust.org.uk
Web site
http://www.princes-trust.org.uk

WORK

TECs – TRAINING AND ENTERPRISE COUNCILS

TECs offer a variety of training courses for unemployed people, school leavers and small businesses. They arrange training for people on a range of government training schemes. Offer careers guidance and educational programmes. And offer advice to small businesses (start-ups) plus financial help for businesses who want to train their staff.

Address	9th Floor, Westminster Tower
	3 Albert Embankment
	London SE1 7SX
Telephone	0171 735 0010
Fax	0171 735 0090

E-mail
tecnc@tecnc.demon.co.uk
Web site
http://www.tec.co.uk

TOMORROW'S PEOPLE TRUST

Helping people back to work

Tomorrow's People Trust is a charity running programmes for the unemployed or underemployed. They aim to help people back into work through counselling and information about training opportunities. The Trust prides itself on an individual approach to every client's needs.

Address	1 Little Argyll Street
	London W1R 5DB
Telephone	0171 287 4500
Fax	0171 287 5767

TRAINING AND EMPLOYMENT AGENCY

To enable people seeking employment to receive the necessary training and jobs

By helping jobseekers to find employment and providing people with relevant skills for work, the Training and Employment Agency aims to create an environment for economic growth in Northern Ireland. The agency, in delivering its services, works in close cooperation with the Industrial Development Board, the Local Enterprise Development Unit, the Industrial Research and Technology Unit and the Northern Ireland Tourist Board. In carrying out its work the Agency is fully committed to supporting the elimination of all forms of discrimination in employment and to using its services to help secure the objectives of fair employment, sex discrimination and disabled persons legislation. It also seeks to ensure equality of opportunity and fair treatment for all in the implementation of its programmes.

Address	Clarendon House
	9-21 Adelaide Street
	Belfast BT2 8DJ
Telephone	01232 541541
Fax	01232 541542

WORK

WORKABLE

Graduate Support Scheme

The Graduate Support Scheme exists to support disabled graduates and students in finding work. The main drive of the scheme is to link clients with employers via temporary work-experience placements. Workable also provides assistance with the preparation of CVs and application forms, and advice regarding interview skills. Workable provides services to employers. These include consultation services, where Workable offers advice with regard to the employment of graduates with disabilities. Disability and Employment Awareness Workshops are also offered as well as advice and assistance with equipment and access needs, advice on the implications of the Disability Discrimination Act and other legislation, and assistance on job design issues. Workable also has European links. Workable Centre Network Europe is a group of organisations working with young disabled people currently offering placements and opportunities in Austria, Germany, Italy, and the Netherlands. Contact by phone during office hours Monday-Friday 9am-5pm.

Address	Premier House
	10 Greycoat Place
	London SW1P 1SB
Telephone	0171 222 8866
Fax	0171 222 1903
E-mail	

info@workable.org.uk

YEAR IN INDUSTRY

Arranges paid gap-year employment and training nationwide

A scheme offering students a pre-degree taste of industry – paid, challenging work in a company, backed by comprehensive 'off-the-job' training. The scheme is designed to stimulate students' interest in industry and to help companies spot future graduate talent and although open to students of any discipline, it is particularly suited to those interested in any branch of engineering, science, computing, mathematics etc – acknowledged shortage skills. If you are expecting, or already have an offer of a place on a degree course, Year in Industry can put you in contact with participating companies – the companies choose who they will interview/employ – and you will spend up to a year gaining experience and learning skills in your chosen discipline. At the end you may be offered sponsorship to do your degree

WORK

course, or you may be offered future employment or summer vacation work with the company. If your placement involves living or working away from home Year in Industry can provide advice and support. 86% of Year in Industry graduates from the pilot scheme returned to industry on completing their degree course – 24% with Firsts, 43% Upper Seconds. Most Admissions Tutors readily support deferred entry.

Regional addresses
Year in Industry has 11 regional offices – contact Head Office at address below for your local details
Costs/waiting lists
No costs. Contact during upper sixth year, 6-12 months before pre-degree starts

Address	Simon Building
	University of Manchester
	Oxford Road
	Manchester M13 9PL
Telephone	0161 275 4396
Fax	0161 275 4396

E-mail
yini@fs3.eng.man.ac.uk
Web site
http://www.yini.org.uk/yini

YOUTHAID

Provides information on rights/opportunities on training, education and employment

Youthaid is a national charity for unemployed young people and provides information on unemployment, benefits, training and employment. Through its publications, Youthaid keeps young people up to date on developments in government legislation and opportunities for training and study.

WORK

Address	322 St John Street
	London EC1V 4NT
Telephone	0171 833 8499
Fax	0171 278 4814

WORK

PUBLICATIONS

GUIDE TO CAREERS AND COURSES IN TRAVEL AND TOURISM, A

The Institute of Travel and Tourism's essential reading for those interested in a career in the travel industry. Available from ITT, 113 Victoria Street, St Albans, Hertfordshire. AL1 3TJ.

Price   £3.00

LIGHTS, CAMERA, ACTION: CAREERS IN FILM, TELEVISION AND VIDEO

Guide to media employment opportunities and career advice

An invaluable guide to media employment opportunities. Gives sound advice on types of job available, qualifications required, recent changes in the industry and first steps along a career path. Useful job profiles and interesting case studies are included. Updated annually. Available from public libraries, bookshops (£9.99) or direct from the address below (price £10.99 inc p&p). BFI Publishing, 21 Stephen Street, London W1P 2LN

Price   £10.99
ISBN   0 85170 343 7

WORKING IN TOURISM – THE UK, EUROPE & BEYOND

This book provides all the information needed by anyone looking for seasonal or permanent employment as guides, company reps, drivers, cabin crew, child-minders, sports instructors, chefs etc, in the tourist industry around the world.

Address	Vacation Work Publications
	9 Park End Street
	Oxford OX1 1HU
Telephone	01865 241 978
Fax	01865 790 885
Price	£9.99
ISBN	1 85458 133 3

WORK

WORKPLACE

Complete guide to work experience placements

Workplace offers practical advice and information for those seeking and organising work placements. Covers work experience, workshadowing and work observation as alternatives, finding placements, preparation, progression, funding, health and safety insurance, accommodation and travel.

Address	Central Bureau for Educational Visits & Exchanges
	10 Spring Gardens
	London SW1A 2BN
Tel	0171 389 4004
Fax	0171 389 4426
Price	£8.99
ISBN	1 89860 107 X

WORK

INFORMATION

This section is designed to introduce CVs, application forms, job search and interview techniques. The information is aimed at giving you the edge in today's job market. Although careers are mentioned throughout this section, the techniques described are equally valid for college, university, and vocational training schemes.

Before looking for work it is essential that you 'know yourself' so that you can decide on the type of job and the industry that you want to work in. The next few pages encourage self-assessment aimed at helping you focus your thoughts more clearly on what you want out of life and from your future career.

WORK

WORK

Skills Check

What's a skills check?

Your skills check will help you focus your thoughts more clearly when thinking about your future career and what direction you want to take. It looks at what you have done and what you feel are your strengths.

Put a tick against all the things that you can do to whatever degree – remember to tick things that you have experienced outside work as well as at work. Also put a tick against the things that you feel particularly good at.

What are my skills?

	What can I do?	What am I good at?
Verbal Communication		
Selling	☐	☐
Public speaking	☐	☐
Telephone	☐	☐
Answering queries	☐	☐
Teaching	☐	☐
Written Communication		
Writing letters or reports	☐	☐
Understanding written reports	☐	☐
Minute- or note-taking	☐	☐
Correcting mistakes	☐	☐
	What can	What am

	I do?	I good at?

Technical
Machine-operating ❑ ❑
Fault-finding ❑ ❑
Maintenance ❑ ❑
Repairs ❑ ❑

Practical
Building ❑ ❑
Woodwork ❑ ❑
Decorating ❑ ❑
Making things ❑ ❑

Administration
Keeping files ❑ ❑
Organising systems ❑ ❑
Organising people ❑ ❑
Dealing with letters ❑ ❑

Numeracy
Accounts ❑ ❑
Cash-handling ❑ ❑
Using maths ❑ ❑
Working out measurements
or quantities ❑ ❑

Mental Ability
Problem-solving ❑ ❑
Thinking of new ideas ❑ ❑
Figures ❑ ❑

WORK

Other

Write down any other skills you feel you have that are not covered by these.

What's next?

Look over what you've ticked. It shows the areas and skills that you already have which will be useful to future employers. It also shows areas that you may want to get involved in or improve.

For any job or area of work that you are interested in try to identify the skills that you think may be needed. Write them down and see how they compare with what you have already

> Try it in your spare time
> Do it on a voluntary basis
> Start to get training

Then:

Write action plans to get information from:

> Your local reference library
> Your careers office/Jobcentre
> Talking to people you know

Work Style

What's my work style?

Everybody has their own opinion of what gives job satisfaction. For example, some people prefer security – although this often means comparatively low pay. Others prefer higher-risk types of work, where there isn't as much security and where pay can be much higher. Most of us tend to choose a compromise between the two.

If you can find out as much about what you want from work as possible, it will help you identify what areas of yourself and your career to work on.

What do I want from work?

Answer all the following questions using the following key:

    Y (for yes) if this is what you do want
or **N** (for no) if you do not mind.

Remember, be honest with yourself – there aren't any right or wrong answers.

PAY	YES	NO
Enough to live on	Y	N
High wages	Y	N
Paid by performance	Y	N
Regular wages	Y	N

WORK

HOURS	YES	NO
Fixed hours	Y	N
Overtime	Y	N
Flexible hours	Y	N
PROSPECTS		
Promotion chances	Y	N
Security	Y	N
LOCATION		
Work near home	Y	N
Work anywhere	Y	N
Based near home but working away	Y	N
Travelling long distances	Y	N
CONDITIONS		
Hot	Y	N
Cool	Y	N
Outdoors	Y	N
Clean workplace	Y	N
OTHER PEOPLE		
Prefer working alone	Y	N
Prefer working in a group	Y	N
Like dealing with the public	Y	N
MANAGEMENT		
Use own initiative	Y	N
Be supervised	Y	N
Manager available if needed	Y	N
DEPTH OF INVOLVEMENT		
Like to develop your abilities	Y	N
See end result	Y	N
OTHER THINGS YOU MAY WANT		
Status	Y	N
To help others	Y	N
To get recognition from others	Y	N

Forming a picture of your working style

Look over the question sheet again. Start to ask yourself questions about some of the answers you have given.

> How do your work style answers reflect your life at the moment?
> How do they match the areas of work you may be interested in?
> What sort of changes in work style would you make to get the right job?
> What would you not change at all no matter what the job?
> Why would you be unprepared to change these?

WORK

The next steps

Having given careful consideration to the previous pages you should now have a clearer idea of what you can offer an employer and also what you want.

Now identify the type of work that you want to research in more depth and compare what you can do with what you want to do.

Using the information you have recorded about yourself, ask yourself the following:

WORK

- What are my current skills?
- Which new skills could I learn?
- Qualifications/training I have or could obtain
- What are my physical attributes?
- What physical conditions do I want to avoid?
- What situations am I comfortable in/wish to avoid?
- What do I want from my job?
- Any personal interests I would like my job to incorporate

Having researched the job you think you would like, ask yourself the following and compare with your personal requirements:

- Which skills does the job require?
- Which skills would need to be learned?
- Which qualifications/training will be required?
- Which physical qualities are required?
- What does the job give me?
- Which of my interests are incorporated?

Job Search

No one can just walk out and get a job. You need to know yourself so that you can choose the right type of job and industry to suit you. You need to have researched that job so that you can develop the skills necessary. Finally you need to be **committed** to finding a job.

Do not just react to advertised vacancies as everybody else will also be applying. Try to be productive and create your own vacancy by using the speculative approach or personal contacts.

WORK

Finding a vacancy

The first step to getting a job is finding a vacancy. Below are listed a few methods of finding vacancies:

1. **Personal contact**
Many vacancies found like this will not have been advertised so there is less competition

2. **Speculative**
Again, these vacancies will not have been advertised. 10% chance of being interviewed using this approach

3. **Agencies**
Check agency is experienced in your type of work and that they usually have vacancies not advertised elsewhere

WORK

4. Newspapers
Local newspapers usually have a specific day for job vacancies

National newspapers – check with your team adviser or employment coordinator for the best newspapers for your type of work

5. Specialist magazines
Many national publications. Often locally published recruiting newspapers/magazines

6. Jobcentres
Vary from area to area

Correct tools

Finding a job is a job in itself and must be approached as such.

You will need the correct tools:

- A quiet place to work
- A copy of your CV
- Scrap paper
- Good quality paper
- Envelopes
- Stamps
- Pens
- A ruler
- A dictionary

Put time aside and send a set number of applications each week. Sending the odd application and waiting for a reply is wasting time.

If you hear nothing after one week telephone to ensure your application has been received. Keep a record of all employers contacted.

WORK

Doing My Application Form

The first contact

The application form is usually your first contact with an employer so, to make the most of every opportunity, you'll want to create a good impression. Here's a checklist of some of the things you should do:

Before starting

- Carefully read all the instructions
- If there is anything you aren't sure of ask someone

Completing the form

- Do a test version on a photocopy or blank piece of paper
- Use a good, black pen
- Write clearly and neatly
- Make sure the spelling is correct
- If you do make a mistake on the final version, use Tippex rather than crossing out
- Keep your answers short and relevant
- Decide what skills the employer is looking for and reflect those skills on the form

After completing it

- Check it carefully
- Make sure dates are correct and that they make sense
- Is it clear which job you are applying for?
- Make a copy of the form – you will need to read it before your interview
- Don't cram the form into a small envelope
- Post the form as soon as possible

REMEMBER: Many people do not complete their forms properly. Because of this they are not selected for interview. There is no need for you to be in that position – give yourself the best chance by taking time and trouble over it.

How do I request an application form?

If an advertisement asks you to write for an application form, do that and no more.

WORK

Example to request an application form

27 Squat View
Stickleback
Near Troutville
Surrey SM99 4BU
Tel: 01324 123456
(your address)

The Personnel Manager
Pearson Perambulators
Nirvana Industrial Complex
Guppy
Essex GU5 1XB
(their address)

1 November 1997

Reference number
(if given in advert)

Dear Sirs,

Sales Assistant

Please forward an application form for the above position as advertised in The Chronicle on 28 December 1997 and, if possible, a job description.

Yours faithfully,

Your signature

S Snurd
(print your name underneath)

Telephone Techniques

Checklist for telephone usage

- **Smile**

- Give all your attention to the call

- Use the person's name

- Prepare a script of your main points

- **Listen** to what the other person says

- Vary the tone and emphasis of your voice

- Be clear and concise

- Do not be frightened of pausing

WORK

Notes on your technique

WORK

Interview Techniques

Preparation

Arrive on time
- Check how long the journey takes
- Make sure you know which department to go to

Do your homework
- Know as much as possible about the organisation
- Find out as much as possible about the job

Know yourself
- Can you outline your life and career clearly?
- Think of examples of your successes and achievements
- Show a positive attitude towards previous employers

What do you want from the interview
- List the information that you want to know

The interview

Initial impressions
- Dress smartly and conventionally
- Find out the interviewer's name from the receptionist
- When entering the room smile, bid them good day and use the interviewer's name

Conversation

- A good interview is a two-way conversation
- Be normal
- Concentrate on what the interviewer is saying

Using the interview to your advantage

- Use every opportunity to speak positively about your past and current work/training
- You should be talking for 60% of the time
- Never answer just 'yes' or 'no'. Expand your answers
- Be clear and precise
- Be positive

After the interview

- If you have heard nothing after one week, telephone
- If unsuccessful try to find out why
- All unsuccessful interviews are practice for the next one – you will eventually be successful

REMEMBER

Enthusiasm
Energy
Experience relevant to the job
Knowledge of the company

WORK

WORK

Responding to interview questions

a) What did you do in your last job?

Explain what your last job involved and include the following points:

- Duties that are relevant to the job you are applying for
- Skills used in the job
- Types of people you dealt with
- Reasons for any promotion
- Areas of responsibility
- Machines and equipment used

b) Why did you leave your last job?

Mention only the reasons that make you look good. If your health was a factor then do not discuss in depth but stress that you are now fit and able to do everything required by the new job.

Many reasons are acceptable to an employer, such as:

- The job was temporary or seasonal
- Part-time
- Deciding to change direction
- Low pay
- Redundancy
- Too much travel
- Unsociable hours

c) Have you ever done this type of work?

Always try to answer positively and explain any experience that shows knowledge and ability. If you have limited or no experience then tell the interviewer about anything else that demonstrates how quickly you can learn. Stress how keen you are to learn.

d) What machines/equipment can you use?

This question applies to all jobs. Mention the following:

- All equipment and experience that would be used in the job applied for. Be precise and use the name and type of equipment if possible
- Experience of any other machines that may be relevant. Again, be precise
- Any relevant machinery used for your hobbies

e) What wage/salary are you looking for?

You will usually be informed of the salary offered. However, this is sometimes negotiable, which can be awkward. If you ask too high a figure you may 'price yourself out'; too low and you could be 'underselling yourself'. Here are some ideas on how to respond:

- Do not specify a figure

WORK

WORK

- Be a little vague, i.e. a fair day's pay for a fair day's work; standard rate for the job is fine; the company has a good reputation so I'm sure the wage/salary will be suitable

If possible, after the interview find out what other workers doing the same job are paid. If you are then offered the job you at least have an idea and will be able to negotiate.

f) Why do you want to work for this company?

You must give positive reasons which suggest you will be loyal to the company. It also provides the opportunity for you to demonstrate that you have researched well prior to the interview – impressive.

g) Did you have much time off during your last job?

If you had very little time off then state that fact in a positive way. If you had a lot of time off then explain the reasons and state why it would not happen in this job.

h) Why should we take you on?

Answer quickly and positively. List your positive attributes, even if this means repeating yourself. Make sure you demonstrate that you are reliable, loyal, efficient, hard-working and capable of doing the job.

i) Do you have good health?

The interviewer is looking for two things here – your fitness for the particular job and your general health.

Try to set his/her mind at rest on both issues:

- If you are in good health, then say so positively
- If you have entered any health information on your application form discuss this but assure the interviewer it will have no detrimental effect on the job applied for and that your general health is good
- Refer to examples that demonstrate you have overcome any disability

j) What are your strengths?

Yet another chance to list your positive qualities. Cover the following:

- Skills
- Pride in doing a good job
- Enthusiasm for the job
- Experience
- Ability to get on well with others
- Interest
- Reliability
- Efficiency

WORK

k) What are your weaknesses?

Never admit to any weaknesses. It is possible to respond as follows:

- I have none that prevent me from being a good worker
- None in relation to this job

l) Tell me more about yourself

This gives you a chance to expand aspects of your personal life. You should demonstrate that you have outside interests; have links between these interests and the job; have normal domestic circumstances.

Mention the following:

- Hobbies/leisure activities
- Clubs of which you are a member
- Position held in any club, etc.
- Past job experience
- Your family
- Brief personal history

m) What did your last employer think of you?

Give a positive answer, mentioning jobs for which you received praise. Stress your efficiency, reliability, punctuality, etc. If you have an open reference from your last employer, then show that. Never criticise previous employers as this gives the impression you may criticise this employer in the future.

n) How old are you?

If you are asked this question then the employer may be worried you are too young or too old for the job. Don't just give your age but point out the advantages and discuss any disadvantages.

WORK

WORK

Curriculum Vitae

Your CV should be aimed at getting an interview and is your selling document.

It should get the employer's:

Attention
Interest
Desire
Action

Things to do when writing it

- Use your **skills check** list
- Use **short** sentences containing facts
- Start with **action** words. For example:
  'Developed a stock control system ...'
  'Gained driving licence ...'
  'Organised work schedules ...'
  Don't start with things like
  'My duties consisted of ...'
- Use **positive** words – see below
- **Any** negative information and you will fail to get an interview

Making it sound positive

Some words to use:

Achieved
Administered
Advised people
Analysed
Arranged events
Benefit
Built
Capable
Competent
Controlled
Created
Designed
Detailed
Developed
Directed

Effective
Efficient
Expanded
Experienced
Guided
Implemented
Improved
Initiated
Involved
Led
Liaised
Maintained
Managed
Monitored
Organised

Outgoing
Participated
Positive
Productive
Proficient
Qualified
Reliable
Repaired
Resourceful
Specialised
Successful
Supervised
Stable
Versatile

WORK

These words may help you when writing about your personal skills – ie, things you believe you are good at, or qualities that you have:

Active
Calculating data
Checking accuracy
Classifying
Coaching people
Compiling
Constructing
Coordinating events
Correspondence
Counselling people
Delegating
Dispensing information
Drafting reports
Editing
Handling complaints

Inspecting
Interpreting data
Interviewing people
Maintaining records
Mediating
Motivating staff
Organising people
Operating equipment
Persuading people
Planning
Preparing charts
Programming computers
Promoting events
Protecting
Raising funds

WORK

Covering Letters

To cover a CV

Your Ref: UT 168

FAO: Personnel Manager

13 North Street
Newbridge
Essex OD2 9PZ
Tel: 01968 446966

1 November 1997

Dear Sir/Madam

PRODUCTION ASSISTANT POST

I was very interested to see your advertisement in the Sunday Times.

I feel positive that my previous work experience and training make me a suitable candidate for the position currently offered. During my five months training on the Drive For Youth Development Programme I have worked hard with a team making me more aware of the needs and sensitivities of others. I have also developed my organisational and planning abilities.

The full breadth of my training and experience is shown in the enclosed CV.

I would be grateful for an interview at your earliest opportunity.

Thank you for your time and attention.

Yours faithfully,

J. Jones

When applying without any previous advertisement

13 North Street
Newbridge
Essex
OD2 9PZ

The Personnel Manager

Tel: 01968 446966

1 November 1997

WORK

Dear Sir/Madam

PRODUCTION ASSISTANT

I am applying for any vacancies in your production department.

During the past five months I have been on the Drive For Youth Development Training Programme. Over this period I have been improving my teamwork, planning, organisation and communication skills. I am very enthusiastic and keen about my work and I believe I have a very approachable character with my work colleagues. I am also well-organised and calm under pressure which will help in dealing with external suppliers and coping with tight schedules.

I enclose my CV and look forward to your reply regarding any current or future vacancies that you feel I may be suited for.

Thank you for your time and attention.

Yours faithfully,

J. Jones

To cover an application form

WORK

Your Ref: UT 168/SMB/jh

Mr C.J. Jameson,
Personnel Manager

13 North Street
Newbridge
Essex
OD2 9PZ

Tel: 01968 446966

1 November 1997

Dear Mr Jameson

PRODUCTION ASSISTANT POST

Please find enclosed my completed application form for the above position as advertised in the Sunday Times.

I am very interested in this position and I am confident that I have the necessary drive and self-motivating approach to my work that you are looking for. I have been developing my interpersonal and organisational skills during my training over the last five months and I am keen and enthusiastic to learn new approaches and develop my abilities.

I am looking forward to meeting you at any interview you may arrange.

Thank you for your time and attention.

Yours sincerely,

J. Jones

WEB SITES

ANSWERING ADS FOR JOBS

Some helpful FAQs on replying to job ads

Web site
http://www.hkjobs.com/info/faq/faq4.html

COMPLETE GUIDE TO THE INTERVIEW

A wealth of information on preparing for a job interview covering almost every query

Web site
http://www.collegeview.com/careers/intervie
wing.html

ECM VACANCY SEARCH

Search for job-specific vacancies by entering key words

Web site
http://www.ecmsel.co.uk/fvac.htm

EMPLOYMENT SERVICES HOME PAGE

Department of DfEE which is responsible for the management of Jobcentres

Web site
http://www.open.gov.uk/dfee/emp/eshome.htm

WORK

WORK

IT JOBS

Provides links to www sites for just about every IT recruitment agency in the UK

Web site
http://www.internet-
solutions.com/itjobs/ukselect.htm

IT JOBSEARCH

Listing of current IT vacancies based on a key skill search engine

Web site
http://www.itjobsearch.com

JOB.NET – JOBLISTINGS

Large listing of jobs in information technology, finance, consultancy, sales etc

Web site
http://www2.vnu.co.uk/jobnet

JOBSERVE – IT VACANCIES

The largest selection of current IT vacancies with a useful search engine

Web site
http://www.jobserve.com

JOBSITE

Jobs on-line within minutes of availability with a search engine based on skills

Web site
http://www.jobsite.co.uk

MATCHMAKER

On-line recruitment service provides contacts for available positions

Web site
http://www.matchmaker.co.uk

MODERN APPRENTICESHIP: TRAINING ORGANISATIONS

Huge listing of industry training organisations also offering careers advice

Web site
http://www.open.gov.uk/dfee/info/maitos.htm

WORK

WORK

MUSIC DIRECTORY

UK's music directory including free ads for musicians/available jobs etc

Web site
http://www.music-media.co.uk

PEOPLE BANK

Database of job vacancies

Web site
http://www.peoplebank.com/pbank/owa/pbk 06w00.main

REED ON-LINE JOBS

Large listing of current vacancies of all descriptions

Web site
http://www.reed.co.uk

RECRUITNET – JOBLISTINGS

A good search engine for current vacancies based on your key skill

Web site
http://recruitnet.guardian.co.uk/index.htm

SELF EMPLOYMENT – SETTING UP YOUR OWN BUSINESS

Information on setting up your own business

Web site
http://www.dss.gov.uk/ca/self-emp.htm

UK RECRUITMENT AND TRAINING

Links to lots of UK Recruitment web pages

Web site
http://www.internet-solutions.com/itjobs/ukselect.htm

UWE CAREERS SERVICE

An extensive database of jobs and graduate recruiters

Web site
http://www.uwe.ac.uk/careers/info/links.htm#ukjobs

WRITING A RESUME

Some helpful FAQs on preparing a résumé

Web site
http://www.hkjobs.com/info/faq/faq1.html

WORK

COMPUTING

WEB SITES

WWW

3DINFO.COM 3D CONSUMER WEB SITE

http://www.3dinfo.com

AVALON 3D RENDERING OBJECTS

http://avalon1.viewpoint.com

GAMELAN JAVA RESOURCES

http://www.gamelan.com

GEOCITIES HTML GUIDE

http://www.geocities.com/athens/2090

IBM

http://www.ibm.com

IRC HELP

http://www.irchelp.org

WWWW

JAVASOFT SUN LEARN JAVA

http://www.javasoft.com

MICROSOFT

http://www.microsoft.com

NETSCAPE

http://home.netscape.com

SUN MICROSYSTEMS

http://www.sun.com

UNIX HELP

http://www.hardrock.org/unixhelp

FILM & TV

WEB SITES

BLOCKBUSTER

http://www.blockbuster.com

CORONA FILMS

http://www.corona.bc.ca/films

DISNEY

http://www.disney.com

EMPIRE

http://www.erack.com/empire

FILMSCOUTS

http://filmscouts.com

HOLLYWOOD ONLINE

http://www.hollywood.com

INTERNET MOVIE DATA BASE

http://www.imdb.com

WWWW

TV LISTING

http://www.yearling.com

FUN, GAMES & SCREEN SAVERS

WEB SITES

ABUSE-A-TRON

http://www.xe.net/upstart/abuse

COMEDY WEB

http://www.comedyweb.co.uk

COMPUTER GAMES WEEKLY

http://www.zdnet.com/cgwuk

DILBERT ZONE, THE

http://www.unitedmedia.com/comics/dilbert

E-ON

http://www.e-on.com

ESCAPE

http://www.escapemag.co.uk

GALTTECH

http://www.galttech.com/ssheaven.shtml

GAMECENTER.COM

http://www.gamecenter.com

GAMERS INN

http://www.gamersinn.com

GAMESDOMAIN

http://www.gamesdomain.co.uk

HAPPY PUPPY

http://www.happypuppy.com

JOKE OF THE WEEK

http://www.dareware.com/jokes.htm

PF MAGIC

http://www.oddballz.com

WWW

SCREEN SAVER A 2 Z

http://www.sirius.com/~ratloaf

WORLD VILLAGE

http://204.96.11.210/kidz

ALTA VISTA EUROPE

http://www.altavista.telia.com

ALTA VISTA

http://www.altavista.digital.com

C | NET SERVICES

http://www.download.com

GEOCITIES

http://www.geocities.com

HOT BOT

http://www.hotbot.com

HOT MAIL

http://www.hotmail.com

INTERNET MAGAZINE

http://www.emap.com/internet

PC ADVISOR

http://www.pcadvisor.co.uk

PC WORLD

http://www.pcworld.com

TU COWS

http://www.tucows.com

YAHOO

http://www.yahoo.co.uk

MUSIC

WEB SITES

.DOTMUSIC

http://www.dotmusic.co.uk

BBC RADIO 1

http://www.bbc.co.uk/radio1

CAPITAL FM

http://www.capitalfm.co.uk

CD NOW!

http://cdnow.com

FLY! MAGAZINE

http://www.cerbernet.co.uk/fky

MINISTRY OF SOUND

http://www.ministryofsound.co.uk

www

MIXMAG ON-LINE

http://www.techno.de/mixmag

NET RADIO

http://www.netradio.net

NME

http://www.nme.com

Q

http://www.erack.com/qweb

SELECT

http://www.erack.com/select

SONY

http://www.sony.com

NEWS

WEB SITES

DAILY TELEGRAPH

http://www.telegraph.co.uk

GUARDIAN

http://www.guardian.co.uk

REUTERS

http://www.reuters.com

TIMES

http://www.the-times.co.uk

UK YELLOW PAGES ONLINE

http://www.yell.co.uk

WWW VIRTUAL LIBRARY

http://www.w3.org/pub/DataSources/bySubject/Overview.html

YAHOO NEWS SITES

http://www.yahoo.com/news

TRAVEL

WEB SITES

AA INSPECTED HOTELS AND RESTAURANTS

http://www.theaa.co.uk/hotels

BRITISH AIRWAYS

http://www.british-airways.com

CAMPUS

http://www.campustravel.co.uk

EUROSTAR

http://www.eurostar.com/eurostar

FERRIES

http://seaview.co.uk/ferries.html

FOREIGN OFFICE TRAVEL ADVICE

http://www.fco.gov.uk/reference/traveladvice/
index.html

INTERNET TRAVEL NETWORK

http://www.itn.net/cgi/get?itn/index

LONELY PLANET

http://www.lonelyplanet.com

NATIONAL EXPRESS COACH

http://www.nationalexpress.co.uk

ROUGH GUIDES

http://www.hotwired.com/rough

STA

http://www.statravel.co.uk

TIME OUT

http://www.timeout.co.uk

WORLD TRAVEL GUIDE

http://www.wtgonline.com

INDEX